VAT and Education

Gillian McGill
Larking Gowen LLP

Published October 2026 by
Spiramus Press Ltd
102 Blandford Street
London
W1U 8AG

www.spiramus.com

Paperback ISBN 9781913507909
Digital ISBN 9781913507916

Contents

Table of cases

Chapter 1: INTRODUCTION

The design of the VAT system works perfectly and simply for businesses that are engaged entirely in one activity, preferably one that is standard rated. As soon as we introduce anything that is within, or potentially within, one of the exceptions to the standard rate, the tax becomes complex.

The education sector has the misfortune of touching upon a multitude of complexities which makes correct reporting of VAT a challenge for those concerned. In addition, VAT requires that decisions are made "in the moment" at the point at which money is received or an invoice raised. As with other sectors, further difficulties arise when dealing with large or unusual transactions, such as land- and property-related matters. These decisions are made across hundreds if not thousands of instances within a VAT period and taxpayers do not have the luxury of having nine months before having to report to HM Revenue and Customs as with corporation tax returns or ten months for income tax self-assessment.

The imposition of VAT to private school fees has highlighted the tax in the public consciousness, but those working across the sector will be well aware that VAT has always been a difficult tax to grapple with and has spawned numerous court cases.

This publication aims to provide guidance to those working within, and advising on, the education sector. It does not, and cannot, provide answers to every possible scenario an organisation faces and is necessarily up to date as at 1 August 2026. Checking that there is no subsequent change in legislation, case law, or HMRC guidance will always be required together with seeking advice from an adviser on the facts specific to the issue at hand.

Information within this book is taken from legislation, HMRC Public Notices, Business Briefs, Guidance Notes, HMRC internal manuals, all of which can be accessed online.

Education providers inevitably undertake more than just core provision of education. Necessarily, this book must cover more than just the education provisions, and address most of the typical activities of an education establishment including land and property lettings, cultural services, and sports activities.

Frequently, disputes arise as to how in practice the VAT law is to be applied to any given scenario. Commercial operations have developed enormously since the 1970s and the bare bones of the law have not kept pace. We are therefore reliant upon the decisions of the courts to help us to understand how the law must be interpreted and applied.

VAT is self-assessed meaning that the taxpayer must themselves determine what they believe to be the correct filing position for their activities and reflect that within their VAT return. Where HMRC disagrees with a filed position, it has the power to open enquiries which will ask questions and request evidence concerning the issue under dispute. Further details as to HMRC powers and compliance more generally is set out in chapter 3.

Even with the most diligent taxpayer and the most cooperative HMRC officer, matters may still not be agreed upon and disputes can then progress to the Tax Tribunals to be litigated. Decisions made here, if still unsatisfactory to one of the parties and with permission to do so, can be further appealed to the Court of Appeal and Supreme Court.

The decisions on points of law of the Upper Tribunal, Court of Appeal, and Supreme Court set binding case law that other taxpayers with the same fact pattern must follow. It is impossible to comment even in passing upon VAT litigation without acknowledging the impact of Brexit given that the UK's VAT system was originally implemented from EU law upon joining the EEC in 1973. This means that we still have a large body of case law precedents which must be followed which were decisions of the CJEU pre-Brexit and therefore determined how the UK must interpret VAT legislation.

On 23 June 2016, the UK voted to leave the European Union throwing doubt over how VAT legislation would be interpreted in a post-Brexit world. A transition period was agreed which ended on 31 December 2020 and since then the UK has become a "third country" for EU VAT purposes. The way in which the EU court influences UK interpretation of the legislative provisions for VAT has subsequently been split into three categories:

1. Disputes relating to periods up to 31 December 2020:
   Remain subject to EU law although the European Union (Withdrawal) Act 2018 may have retrospective effect
2. Disputes relating to periods between 1 January 2021 and 31 December 2023:

Subject to the European Union (Withdrawal) Act 2018 and the Taxation (Cross Border Trade) Act 2018

3. Disputes relating to periods since 1 January 2024: Subject to the Retained EU Law (Revocation and Reform) Act 2023 and any further legislation enacted that might limit application

Simplistically, we continue to rely upon the VAT Act 1994 but subject to changes (largely) in relation to the cross-border movement of goods post-Brexit. So statutory references in this book are to The VAT Act 1994 unless otherwise stated. The Act is now retained EU legislation and the supremacy of EU law is abolished.

As a result, the Court of Justice of the European Union ('CJEU') is no longer the final court of arbitration for UK VAT matters, with the Supreme Court instead being the highest court of appeal. Decisions that are made by the CJEU will increasingly over time have no binding precedent over UK interpretation of VAT legislation as time passes.

The 2023 Act permits the UK higher courts a greater discretion to depart from decisions of the CJEU. In addition, when considering whether to apply EU decisions, the UK courts are to pay regard to any change of circumstances which are relevant to the retained EU law as well as the extent to which the retained EU case law restricts the development of UK law.

In short, this means that in due course we could see different interpretations in the decisions of the courts for pre-transition and post-transition cases.

The repercussions of the Brexit decision are yet to fully play out. In theory, the UK Government is now able to completely re-write the system of VAT should it have the appetite to do so and, whilst that seems highly unlikely, some tinkering has been possible in the post-Brexit period with the introduction of VAT to private school fees.

It is safe to say that VAT matters are unlikely to become straightforward in the near future and good VAT advisors will still be required to guide organisations through the tax. These are definitely "interesting times" to operate in.

Chapter 2: BUSINESS/NON-BUSINESS

VAT is a tax which applies to the supply of goods or services for consideration within the UK by a taxable person acting as such. The Principal VAT Directive 2006/112/EC tells us that:

> "'Taxable person' shall mean any person who, independently, carries out in any place any economic activity, whatever the purpose or results of that activity."

Therefore, any activity undertaken by a taxable person which is **not** an economic activity is non-economic, and is outside the scope of VAT.

The related provision within the VAT Act 1994 is found at section 4:

> "VAT shall be charged on any supply of goods or services made in the United Kingdom, where it is a taxable supply made by a taxable person in the course or furtherance of any business carried on by him."

Therefore, non-business activities fall outside the scope of VAT.

HMRC Public Notice 700 at paragraph 4.6 provides some guidance as to simple non-business situations, with further guidance provided in their internal VAT Business/Non Business manual which acknowledges that there are activities that might not be regarded as business in other circumstances, [but] may be business for VAT purposes.

Many education providers will not consider themselves to be carrying out an economic activity, particularly where they are in receipt of grant funding. However, this is an area where a great deal of debate has occurred, most recently in 2026 involving Colchester Institute Corporation – see below – and is vital to understand so that your organisation can report its VAT profile accurately.

Lord Fisher

Historically, the decision in *Customs and Excise Commissioners v Lord Fisher* [1981] 2 All ER 147 provided the tests relied upon by HMRC in determining whether an activity is carried out for business purposes or not. These were six tests which indicated if the activity was to be treated as a business.

A number of cases heard more recently have superseded the Lord Fisher tests, culminating in HMRC's Business Brief 10/2022 confirming that the tests are no longer being used.

Longridge-on-the-Thames

Although concerned with the recovery of input tax, the decision of *Longridge on the Thames v Revenue and Customs* [2016] EWCA Civ 930 considered whether those costs were linked with an economic (business) activity.

The taxpayer in this case argued that its charges for activities were non-business and therefore non-economic on the basis that they were heavily subsidised and delivered largely by volunteers. The Court of Appeal found that the correct test to apply was to consider whether the organisation was providing goods or services, or exploiting property, for the purpose of obtaining income on a continuous basis. This is an objective test, not dependent upon the intention of the taxpayer.

Wakefield College

The issue of subsidised income streams was considered again in *Wakefield College v Revenue and Customs* [2018] EWCA Civ 952.

The Court of Appeal had to decide whether the provision of Further Education courses to subsidised fee-paying students was an economic activity. In line with the majority of Further Education providers, Wakefield College treated these activities as non-business activities. The decision of the Court finds that just because a payment is made in exchange for a supply does not automatically mean that the supply constitute an economic activity; all the circumstances under which the supply is made must be considered to determine if it is economic.

The main deciding factor for Wakefield College was that its pricing for courses were set by reference to the cost of providing those courses, and not by reference to what the student could afford to pay, distinguishing it from *Borsele* (Case C-520/14) [2016].

HMRC Business Brief 10/2022 set out its view that there are now two tests for determining business as a result of the Wakefield decision:

1. The activity results in a supply of goods or services for consideration
2. The supply is made for the purpose of obtaining income therefrom (remuneration)

Colchester Institute Corporation

The Court of Appeal decision in *Colchester Institute Corporation v HMRC* [2026] EWCA Civ 363 considered again the issue of when grant-funded education provision was a business activity and has most recently (at the time of writing) been found in favour of the taxpayer.

The facts of the case are peculiar to their time but bear summarising to fully understand the decision reached. Colchester Institute College (CIC) had commissioned building works. Although, at the time, it was commonly accepted that the provision of education was a non-business activity, CIC was able to claim input tax incurred on costs upfront and then repay this to HMRC over time as output tax on deemed supplies of non-business education (this mechanism, commonly referred to as Lennartz accounting, is no longer available for use in business/non-business expenditure).

It was therefore critically important to determine the nature of CIC's activities in order to ascertain whether they were non-business activities requiring repayment to HMRC, or not.

The First Tier Tribunal had found that the grant funding received from the EFA and SFA (as it was at the time) was not consideration for the supply of services to students because there was a lack of a link between that funding and the service provided, nor any link between funding and the costs of providing any particular course. As a result, that decision was that the funding fell outside the scope of VAT.

The Upper Tribunal identified four key facts:

1. The funding agreements restricted the funding to courses within a list on the Government's website.
2. The amount paid was by way of formula that was highly specific to CIC's outputs – the number and type of students as well as the number and type of courses.
3. CIC would have to pay back any part of the funding which was not used for supplying the anticipated courses under clawback arrangements.
4. CIC was required to submit an Individualised Learner Record Data report for each student on a monthly basis.

The Upper Tribunal found in favour of CIC that its funding was not received in relation to non-business activities and was, in fact, consideration received for its supplies of education falling within the scope of VAT (although VAT exempt).

HMRC responded by issuing HMRC Business Brief 8/2021. The Brief confirmed that HMRC acknowledged the decision of the Upper

Tribunal but that its policy concerning grant funded education would remain unchanged i.e. that it is non-business and outside the scope of VAT. This left affected organisations with an unprecedented situation; they could choose whether to continue to treat themselves as having non-business activities, or they could choose to follow the CIC decision and treat their grant funding as consideration for exempt business supplies.

HMRC appealed to the Court of Appeal and its judgment was released in March 2026.

The grounds of appeal by HMRC were:

1. The Upper Tribunal misapplied the decision of *Rayon d'Or*
2. There is no direct link between funding received and a supply

Le Rayon d'Or (Case C-151/13) was a French case heard in the CJEU concerning lump sums received by a nursing home. It found that funding provided by the French government from the sickness insurance fund for the provision of care services was consideration for a supply. The Court of Appeal in *CIC* concluded that *Rayon d'Or* was relevant to the facts at hand. *Rayon d'OR* did not involve payment in respect of services provided to a fixed group of recipients identified at the time funding was agreed, but rather it was calculated by reference to the population and needs at a point in time. This formula served as a proxy for the services available to residents and did not preclude the existence of a direct link between payment made and the services provided.

On the second point, the issue came down to whether funding was for certain activities of CIC on the basis that certain conditions would be met, or that it was paying for the supply of education by CIC to eligible students. The Court found that the funding was paid specifically in return for the delivery of education services, CIC was required to provide those services that were defined by the Funding Agencies, and the funding could only be used for the provision of those services.

Clearly, this decision could have implications across the education sector, not just for Further Education colleges. At the time of writing, HMRC had issued Business Brief 3/2026 stating that it would undertake a review of how to proceed following the CIC decision, but that in the meantime, it did not require colleges to change their VAT reporting.

Business

Once an organisation has determined that it has some business activities, it then needs to decide whether the income arising from those activities is taxable or exempt for VAT. Unless there is a relieving provision within the legislation, income will by default be standard rated.

Academies

Academy schools are private education providers operating in England, generally through charities, providing education and being funded in a similar way to local authority schools. Because their provision of education is free of charge to students, they are not in business for the purposes of their education and would therefore ordinarily be unable to recover VAT incurred on costs. In order to provide a level of parity with local authority schools, section 33B was introduced to afford VAT recovery to academies in relation to their non-business activities.

Academies submit claims to recover VAT using form VAT126 which can be submitted monthly to improve cashflow. This form bears little relation to a VAT return, requiring listing out for each cost being claimed:

- the invoice date;
- the supplier's VAT registration;
- the VAT amount;
- the name of the organisation receiving goods or services on the invoice; and
- a brief description of goods or supplies

It is important to note that the s33B provision covers recovery of VAT on the **non-business activities** only. Academies that are diversifying into income generating activities will need to consider the VAT treatment of these which will mean restricting the recovery of VAT on general overhead costs and costs directly attributable to the income stream, and in some cases, might require that the academy registers for VAT and undertakes partial exemption calculations.

Multi-academy trusts are legally one entity operating across multiple academies. For these, the likelihood of breaching the VAT registration threshold is much higher as the income from all non-core activities within academies in the trust needs to be consolidated and compared to the registration threshold. Multi-academy trusts that include secondary schools are more likely to breach the registration threshold due to the increased facilities at larger sites and therefore the likelihood of these being let etc. Once registered, one VAT return is submitted encompassing all academies within the trust. This return still benefits from s33B recovery of non-business costs, but also treats business income and expenditure in line with any other VAT registered organisation. This means that, once VAT registered, the only restriction the academy makes to its VAT recovery is for its exempt activities (see Chapter 4: Partial Exemption).

Chapter 3: VAT REGISTRATION

Identifying when an organisation needs to be registered for VAT is crucial to maintaining good governance and mitigating the chance of penalties being incurred.

An organisation will be required to register when the value of its taxable supplies exceeds the VAT registration threshold applicable at that point in time.

Effective dates	Registration thresholds £
1 April 2024 -	90,000
1 April 2017 – 31 March 2024	85,000
1 April 2016 – 31 March 2017	83,000

Taxable supplies are those business activities that generate income which would be charged to VAT at the standard rate (currently 20%), reduced rate (currently 5%), or at the zero rate, all being "taxable" rates. We therefore ignore any non-business activities and income arising from exempt activities. The previous chapter considers what is "business" and the following chapters cover the typical exemptions applicable in the sector. By default, any income arising from business activities will be subject to the standard rate of VAT unless otherwise relieved within the legislation; if in doubt, it is standard rated.

The total of income from taxable activities (those subject to 20%, 5%, and the zero rate) needs to be monitored to identify if it exceeds the registration threshold. A breach of the threshold can occur in two ways: either, most commonly, a historic look back to the preceding 12 months, or a look forward to the upcoming 30 days.

Historic test

An unregistered organisation needs to keep monitoring its taxable income on a rolling 12 month basis; this is tricky because the period of breach may not coincide with the organisation's reporting year end or even a quarter end, hence is easy to miss.

Once a breach is identified, the organisation must apply to HMRC for registration by the end of the following month and will be registered from the first of the month after.

> **EXAMPLE:**
>
> Taxable income over the preceding 12 months breaches the threshold in June 2026
>
> HMRC must be notified by submitting a registration application by 31 July 2026
>
> The organisation will be registered for VAT with an effective date of 1 August 2026
>
> Its first VAT return will cover a period commencing 1 August 2026 and VAT must be charged correctly from this date

This means that the income which caused the registration breach is never actually subject to VAT, only the taxable income arising after the effective date of registration.

Future test

If the organisation has an expectation that the value of income from its taxable supplies in the next 30 days alone will exceed the registration threshold, it must notify HMRC by submitting an application to register before the end of the 30 day period and will then be registered with effect from the start of the 30 days.

> **EXAMPLE:**
>
> On 10 June 2026, an organisation realises its upcoming taxable income in the next 30 days will breach the VAT threshold
>
> HMRC must be notified by submitting a registration application by 9 July 2026
>
> The organisation will be registered for VAT with an effective date of 10 June 2026
>
> Its first VAT return will cover a period commencing 10 June 2026 and VAT must be charged correctly from this date

This means that the income which caused the registration breach under the future, look forward test is subject to VAT. This scenario is less common than a historic breach and would generally only arise where there is a large (probably one-off) transaction.

Voluntary registration

Even where a breach has not occurred, and may never do, an organisation can submit an application to register for VAT voluntarily. This might be beneficial where more VAT is being incurred on costs than would be payable on income, particularly where there is a large amount of zero rated income in the organisation.

A voluntary registration could also be made where no taxable income has been generated, but where there is an intention that this will happen in the future. These applications do require that HMRC is given strong evidence of the intentions of the organisation's future taxable income – perhaps through business plans outlining the future profile – as the VAT registration will be recovering more VAT than it pays over, at least until the intentions materialise and income starts to be received. A voluntary registration could be beneficial where, for example, a large building project is being undertaken with VAT-bearing costs being incurred for months or years before any taxable income starts to be generated. The organisation can submit VAT returns claiming repayment of the VAT it has incurred on costs in the periods before it starts to earn income. The ability to recover VAT on costs is always predicated upon the intention to use those costs to make taxable supplies.

It is also possible to apply for registration where the organisation is, or will be, making supplies to recipients outside the UK as long as that income would be taxable (and not exempt) if it were being earned in the UK. This might be applicable and beneficial for organisations that are established in the UK but are predominantly supplying their services to non-UK businesses, such as consultancy to an overseas educator.

VAT returns

Once registered, an organisation will be required to submit VAT returns on a quarterly, monthly, or annual basis. Most organisations will be on a quarterly reporting pattern unless they request monthly reporting and, usually, can demonstrate that they are regularly in a repayment position. Annual returns are available on application but only for organisations with taxable turnover of £1.35 million or less, these organisations are then required to make interim payments towards an estimated VAT liability.

Academies that are not VAT registered make claims to recover VAT on their costs that are attributable to their non-business activities. Claims are made by submission of a form VAT126 to the Trust's Government Gateway account and these can be made monthly which will assist cashflow. The only information required for these claims is:

- the invoice date;
- the supplier's VAT registration;
- the VAT amount;
- the name of the organisation receiving goods or services on the invoice; and
- a brief description of goods or supplies usually provided in an uploaded spreadsheet.

It is important to remember that Academies cannot recover input VAT on costs that relate to any business activities (those that are income generating) under the VAT 126 procedure and, unless there are absolutely no business activities being undertaken, an apportionment will need to be made to calculate the recoverable, non-business proportion of non-attributable mixed use VAT. For most Academies, VAT recovery on these mixed-use costs will still be in the upper ninety percent range.

For registered organisations, the information that is submitted to HMRC is simply the nine boxes of a standard UK VAT return.

Box 1	Output VAT being the UK VAT due on supplies made by the organisation (less any credit notes issued)
Box 2	VAT due on acquisition of goods made in Northern Ireland from EU member states. In practise, unlikely to be required by the majority of education organisations
Box 3	Total of boxes 1 and 2
Box 4	UK VAT reclaimed in the period on purchases, restricted for any non-business or partial exemption calculations
Box 5	Net amount due for payment or repayment being box 3 minus box 4
Box 6	The net value of all supplies made including any income that is exempt or zero rated

Box 7	The net value of all purchases made excluding salaries, loans, tax, or other expenditure that is outside the scope of VAT
Box 8	Value of supplies of goods from Northern Ireland to EU member states. In practise, unlikely to be required by the majority of education organisations
Box 9	Value of acquisitions of goods from EU member states to Northern Ireland. In practise, unlikely to be required by the majority of education organisations

Since 1 April 2022 making tax digital ('MTD') was a mandatory requirement for all VAT registered organisations. This means the organisations must keep digital records and use MTD-compatible software to submit VAT returns. In addition, the payment of any VAT due to HMRC must be made electronically with both the return and payment being submitted by one month and seven days after the period to which they relate.

Late filing of a return will result in a penalty point being issued and once a points threshold is reached, a financial penalty will be issued. Late payment of VAT will result in a financial penalty being applied which increases the later that payment. Interest is also applied to late payment. These are a disincentive to organisations who might otherwise use late payment to HMRC to help finance their activities.

Submission of a VAT return showing a repayment being due to the taxpayer will be checked by HMRC before repayment is released which it aims to process within 30 days. If it is not usual for your organisation to be in a repayment, HMRC is likely to issue a pre-credibility check which is currently facilitated initially by way of a standard questionnaire. Typically, the organisation will be asked about the circumstances giving rise to a repayment and for copies of the larger purchase invoices that are being claimed.

Record keeping

Organisations are required to keep business records for at least six years. Specifically, for VAT purposes, this must include the organisation's VAT account and VAT invoices. HMRC Public Notice 700/21 sets out the requirements of the electronic account, summarised below.

You must have a digital record of:

- your business name

- the address of your principal place of business
- your VAT registration number
- any VAT accounting schemes that you use

Supplies made and received

For each supply, you must record the:

- time of supply — the tax point
- value of the supply — the net value excluding VAT
- rate of VAT charged

The electronic record must also record any adjustments or corrections made to the VAT return.

Self assessment

VAT is a self-assessed tax and every return submission requires a declaration that the organisation believes the reported position to be correct, therefore any errors that later come to light must be corrected. It is possible to make corrections for incorrect reporting either on supplies or on purchases within the preceding four years from the:

- end of the prescribed accounting period in which the error occurred for under-declared and over-declared output tax and over-claimed input tax; or
- due date of the return for the prescribed accounting period in which the error occurred for under claimed input tax

These time limits do not apply if the error was made deliberately, rather than carelessly.

Error correction

Once an error is discovered, it needs to be quantified together with any other errors and reported either within the next VAT return or by separate notification to HMRC. The method for reporting depends upon the quantum of all errors identified:

- Where the net value of errors in previous returns is:
    - not in excess of £10,000, or
    - is between £10,000 and £50,000 but does not exceed 1% of the box 6 value for the current return during which the error is discovered,

  the error can be made by adjusting the current return.

- Where the net value of errors in previous returns is:
    - over £50,000, or
    - between £10,000 and £50,000 but exceeds 1% of box 6, or
    - has been made deliberately,

  the error must be notified to HMRC via a letter or online submission of form VAT 652.

No organisation aims to make mistakes but identifying any that have happened and putting them right should be the focus of maintaining good tax compliance. Penalties can be applied by HMRC when an organisation gets its VAT reporting wrong, but these can be mitigated entirely by correcting the error without being prompted to do so by HMRC and by demonstrating that the organisation has taken "reasonable care" in its VAT reporting.

Chapter 4: PARTIAL EXEMPTION

As mentioned at the start of this book, VAT works generally smoothly and simply for the majority of organisations that generate (or intend to generate) only taxable, business income from their supplies. These businesses account to HMRC for VAT on income but can offset that with the VAT that they have incurred on costs, so that only the net amount is payable to HMRC or repayable by HMRC.

EXAMPLE:

Sales:

Net	1,000
VAT	200

Purchases:

Net	100
VAT	20

VAT payable to HMRC £200 less £20 = £180

If an organisation does not have entirely business taxable income, then its VAT profile will be more complex. VAT incurred on costs will need to be attributed between the organisation's activities, identifying those costs that were incurred:

1. Wholly for its non-business activities
2. For both its non-business and business activities
3. Wholly for its business taxable activities
4. Wholly for its business exempt activities
5. For both taxable and exempt activities

For all but the most straightforward organisations, setting up a robust VAT chart of accounts setting out which transactions fall into each of the categories above, will be necessary to ensure accurate VAT reporting.

VAT incurred wholly for non-business activities

This VAT is not recoverable at all. For this reason, organisations with non-business activities need to be cognisant of the fact that their costs will be 20% more than perhaps expected. This is especially important if relying upon grant funding to pay for an activity; the irrecoverable VAT on costs will need to be included in the amount of funding being applied for.

For both its non-business and business activities

Only VAT incurred in relation to business activities is potentially recoverable, so a method for apportioning mixed use costs needs to be established. There is no set way to calculate how much of mixed use VAT can be allocated to business activities, but whatever method is used must give a fair and reasonable result. This calculation must take place before then dealing with VAT incurred on business activities.

HMRC sets out an example of calculating the apportionment of mixed use VAT on costs by reference to the proportion of business income to total income (so including grants and donations, for example). This may work for organisations for which grants and donations are a good proxy for their non-business activities, but will not necessarily be appropriate for all organisations with non-business activities. HMRC also notes that other methods could include time spent by employees (probably requiring some time recording system to be in place) or floor areas of a mixed use building (although this methodology has been successfully challenged by HMRC in recent cases). For Further Education colleges, a non-business apportionment could be undertaken by reference to the number of full-time equivalent learners that are fully funded versus the total number of full-time equivalent learners.

As stated, whatever method used, the organisation must be satisfied that a fair and reasonable result arises and one that can be evidenced to, and audited by, HMRC.

The business proportion result of applying the business/non-business calculation to mixed use VAT is then taken forward to the next stage: partial exemption.

Wholly for its business taxable activities

The VAT incurred on costs incurred wholly for the organisation's business taxable activities – so those that generate income subject to 20%, 5%, and zero rate VAT – is recoverable in full. This VAT can therefore be included in Box 4 of the organisation's VAT return and is netted off against the output VAT it is paying over to HMRC in Box 3.

Wholly for its business exempt activities

Again, being able to identify those costs that are incurred wholly for the organisation's exempt activities is crucial in ensuring that it reports its VAT correctly. This VAT is *prima facie* not recoverable unless it falls within very small *de minimis* limits – see below. For an education provider, given that their main activity will likely be the provision of exempt or non-business education, there is likely to be a large amount of VAT on costs that falls to be restricted from recovery; this is certainly the case for Further Education providers.

For both taxable and exempt activities

The costs that are identified as relating to the organisation's business but not wholly to either its taxable income or its exempt income generation; this VAT is known as residual or unattributable input tax. The sorts of costs that will fall within this category often includes professional fees of running the organisation, utilities, and other building costs of mixed use space.

Unless something else has been formally agreed with HMRC, calculating the recoverable proportion of this residual VAT must be undertaken by reference to the value of taxable income as a percentage of the total business income; known as the partial exemption standard method.

EXAMPLE:	£
An organisation has the following income:	
Grant income	500,000
Taxable income	10,000
Exempt income	30,000
It incurs VAT on costs as follows:	
Non-business activities	10,000
Taxable business activities	2,000
Exempt business activities	5,000
Mixed use	50,000

As it undertakes both business and non-business activities, it must apportion its mixed use VAT on costs: Business income/Total income	40,000/540,000 = 8% x 50,000 = 3,703
As it generates both taxable and exempt income, it must further apportion its mixed use VAT on costs using the partial exemption standard method: Taxable income/Taxable plus exempt income (rounded up to the next whole number)	10,000/40,000 = 25% x 3,703 = 926
The VAT on costs that is recoverable is the total of that incurred wholly on taxable activities plus the calculated proportion of mixed use VAT:	2,000 + 926 = 2,926 recoverable
The organisation should then consider whether the VAT incurred on its exempt business activities is so small as to fall within the de minimis limits:	3,703 – 926 = 2,777 + 5,000 = 7,777
For this VAT to be recoverable it must be BOTH:	Less than £625 per month on average, and Less than half of your total input tax in the relevant period
In our example, the exempt input tax of £7,777 is not within the *de minimis* limits and so cannot be recovered. **Out of the total £67,000 of VAT incurred on its costs, only £2,926 can be recovered by this organisation.**	

It is possible to agree different methodologies of calculating VAT recovery with HMRC, either a combined method or a special method (see below).

Annual adjustment

Partial exemption calculations are carried out to inform the VAT return position filed on a quarterly (or monthly) basis. These are, however, only a provisional recovery position until the annual adjustment is undertaken which confirms the VAT recovery for the "longer period", usually being the VAT year ended 31 March, 30 April, or 31 May depending on the return stagger. The longer period end can be drawn up to a different date, say 31 July or 31 August, if that is more sensible for the organisation but needs written notification to HMRC of the intention to use a different VAT year end.

For a new VAT registration, the longer period will run from the date of registration to the VAT year end and so possibly will be less than a year in length.

The annual adjustment intends to smooth any fluctuations in VAT recovery throughout the year, for example where the organisation is within the *de minimis* limits for some periods but not all. The partial exemption position is recalculated, still using income as the driver for recovery, but using the values for the whole year.

All the steps above are carried out using the income and expenditure for the entire longer period to arrive at a value for how much VAT should have been recovered. This value is then compared to how much VAT was recovered in the returns filed, with the difference being either paid back to, or claimed from, HMRC by inclusion within Box 4.

Annual recoverable amount	£18,000.50
Provisional amount reclaimed in returns	£22,000.00
Annual adjustment (to HMRC)	£3,999.50

The annual adjustment amount (if there is one) can be included in either the last VAT return of the VAT year, or in the first VAT return of the next VAT year. For most organisations, reporting three months later gives sufficient time to consider the annual adjustment at a very busy time for finance teams.

Standard method override

Since 2002, a requirement to stand back and consider whether the standard income-based method of calculating VAT recovery is fair and reasonable, has been in place, known as the standard method override (SMO).

The SMO addresses the fact that using income received in the VAT year is a crude proxy for calculating the use of costs, particularly in cases where there is a timing difference between income being received and costs being used – for example, where education is provided in one VAT year but has been invoiced in a different VAT year.

We therefore have to apply the SMO at the end of the longer period each year when calculating the annual adjustment. The SMO will impact where an organisation uses the standard income-based method to calculate its VAT recovery and where its residual, mixed use input tax is more than £50,000 per year (i.e. pro rated for longer periods that are not one year). The first step, therefore, is to identify how much VAT on mixed use costs has been incurred in the longer period (this will have been part of the partial exemption calculations). If the £50,000 threshold is not breached, the SMO does not apply.

For organisations with more than £50,000 of residual input tax, further calculations need to be undertaken to establish whether an SMO adjustment bites or not.

The VAT recovery for the longer period should be recalculated on a "use based" method, and then the result compared to the standard method. Where the difference between the two is:

- more than £50,000, or
- at least £25,000 and is 50% of the residual input tax,

then the organisation must report its annual adjustment using the SMO method, not the income-based method. It should be noted that the SMO can improve the VAT recovery position of the organisation and this is a valid basis for reporting.

EXAMPLE:

A university ('EdUni') makes both exempt education supplies and taxable supplies such as catering, commercial research and conferences. It incurs residual input tax of £1,200,000 in a VAT year. Taxable supplies total £10m and total supplies £50m.

Step 1 – Standard Method Calculation:

Recoverable residual input tax = £1,200,000 × (10m / 50m) = £240,000. Total VAT recoverable under the standard method = £150,000 direct + £240,000 residual = £390,000.

Step 2 – Assessment of Fairness:

EdUni determines that actual taxable use of overheads is 35% based on internal cost driver data.

Use-based recovery = £1,200,000 × 35% = £420,000.

Difference = £180,000, exceeding the HMRC override thresholds (£50,000 or 50% of residual and at least £25,000).

Step 3 – Standard Method Override Applied:

Revised VAT recovery: £150,000 direct + £420,000 residual = £570,000.

HMRC provides very little guidance on how it will approach the SMO but does state that if an SMO adjustment is required year on year, it is an indication that the organisation needs to approach HMRC to agree a special method for calculating its VAT recovery.

Partial exemption special method

For some organisations, income is not a good measurement of how it consumes the VAT incurred on costs; where this is the case, it is possible to approach HMRC to agree a different method of calculating the recoverable proportion of residual business VAT. Any calculation that does not use the standard income-based method will, by default, be a special method and require HMRC agreement.

In order to obtain a special method, it is necessary to demonstrate to HMRC why the standard method does not provide a fair and reasonable result and why the proposed method does so. Part of the application to HMRC must include a signed declaration that the organisation considers its proposed special method to provide a fair and reasonable result.

HMRC acknowledges that for Further Education and Higher Education providers, there are particularly complex VAT profiles to consider. They have published a standard framework of agreements, the use of which should make it easier to obtain agreement to a special method than might otherwise be the case. The Partial Exemption HMRC manual sets out the agreed framework labelled as for Higher Education institutions but notes that many of the issues are pertinent to Further Education providers too.

Due to the way that Higher Education students in England pay for their courses at a rate fixed by central government, HMRC is unlikely to accept that the partial exemption standard method gives a fair and reasonable result for HE institutions. This is because the "income" from student fees is subsidised by government grant and so does not provide a fair proxy for the consumption of VAT on costs, therefore requiring the partial exemption override to be regularly invoked which indicates that an income-based method is inappropriate.

HMRC has worked with representatives of universities to agree the framework that Higher Education providers can chose to rely upon in calculating VAT recovery, although the organisation will still need formal HMRC agreement to use the method. The framework is available on HMRC's website with the latest published version being dated August 2020. At the time of writing, HMRC was due to issue new guidance on business/non-business for universities.

In addition, Higher Education organisations will undertake research activities as a large part of their activities and the treatment of this is particularly complicated to administer in practise. HMRC's guidance is sparing in this area but it does separate out commissioned research (business) from that which is university-led research (non-business). University-led research is generally funded by the Research Councils and the results of that work are publicly available, rather than provided to the commissioner as in the case of commissioned research.

European Commission framework funding has been agreed by HMRC to be zero rated income where it is provided under Frameworks 4, 5, or 6 and giving full recovery of costs where fee paying students are not involved in the research. Where fee paying student are involved in the research, costs will become residual as relating to both the zero-rated Framework income and the exempt education provided to those students, unless they are acting as employed research assistants.

Being able to both categorise each research project and then identify and attribute the costs involved requires a robust understanding of the organisation and its systems, therefore obtaining specialist technical assistance in this area would be advisable.

Combined method

Rather than separately calculating both the business/non-business apportionment AND then the partial exemption apportionment, it is possible to agree a combined method with HMRC. This compresses the two steps into one calculation and can only be applied with HMRC agreement. In addition, utilising a combined method removes the ability to claim VAT that falls into the *de minimis* limits.

Chapter 5: CAPITAL GOODS SCHEME

In the same way that an organisation's recovery of VAT is provisional throughout its VAT year until it is confirmed by undertaking a longer period adjustment (annual adjustment), the recovery of VAT on certain capital expenditure is also subject to review under the Capital Goods Scheme ('CGS'). Legislation requiring that organisations perform adjustments of certain capital items is located in the VAT Regulations 112 – 116.

The current CGS rules bite on expenditure of £250,000 (net) on land and buildings, and on expenditure of £50,000 (net) on computer equipment, aircraft, or boats.

£250,000 threshold: This could be buying, constructing, extending, refurbishing, or altering property so will have wide application. This expenditure must be reviewed over ten "intervals" – nine to ten years.

This covers:

- Land
- A building or part of a building
- A civil engineering work or part of a civil engineering work

£50,000 threshold: This expenditure must be reviewed over five "intervals" – four to five years.

This covers:

- A computer or an item of computer equipment
- An aircraft
- A ship, boat, or other vessel

The Government announced changes to the CGS in April 2025, namely that computers would be removed from the scheme and that the land and property threshold would be increased to £600,000 (net) and this was confirmed in HMRC Business Brief 7/2026 to take effect from 29 July 2026. Importantly, any existing CGS items remain within the preceding rules. The new limit for land and property spend applies where the land or property was acquired on or after 29 July, or expenditure incurred on or after 29 July. It will take some time therefore for the benefits of the increased threshold to be seen in practice. These changes are welcome especially given that the application to computer equipment is rarely relevant in current times.

For expenditure to be subject to the CGS, it must:

1. Be at or above the CGS threshold for that type of expenditure
2. Have been capitalised in the accounts of the organisation
3. Have been incurred for at least some business use (if the expenditure is entirely for non-business purposes, it is not within the scope of the CGS)
4. Have incurred VAT

Where these factors are present, the organisation must maintain CGS records and review the use of that asset annually in order to consider whether an adjustment to its original VAT recovery is required. The review period commences when the CGS asset is first brought into use, which could be many months or years after the expenditure started to be incurred.

One of the hardest aspects of the CGS is identifying when the threshold has been breached. This is especially true where expenditure has been incurred in stages or from various suppliers. Awareness of the existence of the scheme and the need to keep a cumulative total of spend is crucial within the organisation.

HMRC's Notice 706/2 sets out its views of how the CGS operates. Notably, HMRC states that:

> "if you've purchased land and constructed a building on it, this is treated as one capital item."

Where a project has multiple stages, it can be less clear whether the CGS threshold has been breached, or not. As a rule of thumb, engaging one contractor under one agreement will point to all the expenditure being considered as one sum. Whereas, HMRC accepts that there can be a phased spend not requiring cumulation where there are separate contracts for each stage of the work, or where each stage is a separate option with one phase completing before the next commences.

Making the CGS adjustment

Expenditure is incurred over time and the VAT on it is recovered in accordance with the intended use of that spend at the time incurred. A record needs to be maintained of the expenditure and the amount of VAT recovered. When the asset is then first brought into use, its CGS life starts.

The first CGS interval will end at the VAT year end of the period when the first use occurred.

> **EXAMPLE:**
>
> Expenditure incurred in December 2025, April 2026, August 2026.
>
> First use September 2026.
>
> CGS period of adjustment commences September 2026.
>
> First CGS interval will be the VAT year that ends in 2027.
>
> Nine further intervals will occur until the CGS life ends.

Importantly, first use will include where the land or property is let out, as well as the organisation's own occupation. It is therefore necessary to be aware when a new lease is granted where the land or property is a CGS item.

Regulation 115 sets out the calculation for land and property spend that must be made each interval:

$$\frac{\text{Total input tax on the capital sum}}{10} \times \text{the adjustment percentage}$$

For other CGS items, the VAT on the capital sum is divided by 5.

The "adjustment percentage" is the difference between the original level of VAT recovery compared to the level of taxable use in the interval. The result can be either an amount due to HMRC, an amount due back to the organisation, or no change. This adjustment, if there is one, is included in Box 4 of the second return following the end of the VAT year.

> **EXAMPLE:**
>
> VAT of £100,000 has been incurred on a new building that will be used for both taxable and exempt education.
>
> At the time it was incurred, the organisation's residual recovery rate was 75% so that £75,000 was recovered.
>
> The building was first used in September 2025 and the organisation's VAT year ends July 2026, being interval one for CGS.
>
> In the VAT year to July 2027, the residual recovery rate for the organisation was 80%.
>
> Its CGS adjustment for that year is:
>
> £100,000/10 = £10,000 x 5% = £500 of additional VAT to recover in Box 4 of the VAT return ending January 2028.

Chapter 6: EDUCATION EXEMPTION

The most important relieving provision for the education sector is within Schedule 9, Group 6 Education:

1. The provision by an eligible body of
   a) Education, or
   b) Vocational training
2. The supply of private tuition, in a subject ordinarily taught in a school or university, by an individual teacher acting independently of an employer
3. The provision of examination services
   a) By or to an eligible body, or
   b) To a person receiving education or vocational training which is
      a. Exempt by virtue of 1 or 2 above [5 or 5A], or
      b. Provided otherwise than in the course or furtherance of a business.

An eligible body for the purposes of this exemption is:

- a school (including private schools), sixth form college, tertiary college or Further Education college or other centrally funded Further Education institution (defined as such under the Education Acts)
- a centrally funded Higher Education institution in Wales, Scotland and Northern Ireland (defined as such under the Education Acts)
- the governing body of one of these institutions:
  - a local authority
  - a government department or executive agency
  - a non-profit making body that carries out duties of an essentially public nature similar to those carried out by a local authority or government department
  - health authority
- a non-profit making organisation that meets certain conditions
- a commercial provider of tuition in English as a foreign language, in which case special rules will apply
- a university

- a Higher Education provider registered in the approved (fee cap) category of the register maintained by the Office for Students from the date of inclusion in the register

These implement EU Article 132(1)(i) requirements for member states to exempt education but by referencing the types of organisations that are found in the UK delivering education. Whether the UK has correctly implemented the EU law has been subject to challenge in a few cases, most recently in *St Patrick's College and others v CRC* [2025] STC 752 which questioned whether commercial providers of education leading to qualifications should benefit from exemption. Notably, the returns that the case concerned were within the pre-Brexit period.

The Court of Appeal has found in favour of the taxpayer concluding that the critical test is how the customer views their learning experience and where a typical student would consider the supplies they receive from a commercial provider to be sufficiently similar to those supplied by an exempt provider, then exemption must apply in order to achieve fiscal neutrality.

We have subsequently had HMRC Business Brief 9/2026 in response to this decision. Importantly, HMRC has been given leave to appeal to the Supreme Court so this remains somewhat unsettled territory for the time being. Until this matter is fully concluded, independent providers of higher education and/or further education, particularly those delivering HNC, HND or degree pathways, should consider whether to submit a claim now that will protect their position pending the Supreme Court decision.

From 1 January 2025, for private schools, the supplies of education and vocational training are taxable at the standard rate of VAT. This does not remove private schools from being eligible bodies if they otherwise would be. It just removes the exemption from their supplies of education and vocational training. Part 3 "Exceptions" was introduced to Schedule 9 which states:

> 1 The provision of education by a private school, other than—
>
> a) (the provision of the teaching of English as a foreign language,
>
> b) the provision of education in a nursery class, or
>
> c) the provision of a Higher Education course.

2 The provision of vocational training by a private school.
3 The provision of board and lodging which is closely related to a supply of a description falling within item 1 or 2.

This change made it critically important to understand what a "school" for the purposes of the VAT legislation is. The Education Act 1944 defines a school as:

> "an institution for providing primary or secondary education or both primary and secondary education, being a school maintained by a local education authority, an independent school, or a school in respect of which grants are made by the Minister to the proprietor of the school."

Simply providing courses to under-16s is not sufficient to be a "school" unless that provision is full-time education suitable for under-16s.

What is education?

In the absence of any definition for education in the legislation, the word takes its ordinarily understood meaning.

HMRC's Education Notice states its view that:

> Education means a course, class or lesson of instruction or study in any subject, regardless of when and where it takes place.
>
> Education includes:
>
> - lectures
> - educational seminars
> - conferences and symposia
> - recreational and sporting courses
> - distance teaching and associated materials
>
> If a separate charge is made for registration, this is part of the provision of education.
>
> Education does not include admission to events such as:
>
> - plays
> - concerts
> - sports meetings
> - exhibitions

EU Directive 2006/112/EC at Article 132(i) specifies exemption for:

> "the provision of children's or young person's education, school or university education, vocational training or retraining, including the supply of services and of goods closely related thereto…"

This extends the exemption beyond the education provided in a formal setting. The EU provisions were considered in the case of *North of England Zoological Society v C & E Commrs* [1999] BVC 437 which found that admission charges to Chester Zoo could be exempt education. The charity included education in its charitable objects and employed a number of dedicated education workers. The judgment referenced the fact that:

> "The word 'education', like many English words, can be used in different senses. It is capable of being used in a general sense of 'broadening the mind'."

HMRC's Education Manual references that "instruction" is key to the existence of education, noting that simply supervision or facilitation are not sufficient. Specifically, HMRC acknowledges that education can include holiday, sporting, and recreational courses where these involve tuition. Instruction is relatively easy to demonstrate in a live learning environment but can be more difficult where learning takes place online.

Distance learning

Increasingly, education is provided in non-traditional ways and the use of online provision has grown exponentially in the 2020s. The extent to which all types of distance learning falls within the education exemption is probably not fully tested yet. Broadly, HMRC takes the view that entirely automated online provision is a digital service, whereas online learning with some element of human interaction is capable of falling within the education exemption depending upon the provider meeting the eligible body condition.

Automated online learning provision can fall to be treated as an electronically supplied service. In these cases, where non-UK learners are receiving supplies, this can create a requirement for the provider to VAT register overseas where those learners are established. Where registration obligations arise in multiple EU countries, a simplification to reporting is available, the One-Stop Shop, which reduces the need for more than one registration and return to report all supplies made to EU consumers.

Further changes were implemented from 1 January 2025 whereby the EU now treats even live online education, webinars, and interactive training and subject to local VAT requiring registration in those countries of receipt, or by using a One-Stop Shop registration. Unhelpfully, this treatment is at odds with the UK position which treats live education as supplied where the provider is established, and potentially leads to double taxation.

Where there is a variety of supplies provided under the distance learning arrangements, whether this is a single supply or multiple supply would need to be determined in order to arrive at a conclusion on the VAT liability of income arising.

HMRC acknowledges that, typically, online learning can comprise a variety of supplies:

- written material (whether in printed or electronic form);
- access to tutorial support;
- student assignments (including whether these are marked and the extent to which feedback is given to students);
- classroom training; and
- any examination or accreditation services.

Although not specifically concerned with distance learning, the case of *College of Estate Management* (2005 UKHL 62) examined the provision of textbooks and whether these were a standalone zero rated supply or formed an ancillary part of the course of learning for students. When reviewing the treatment of packaged supplies, the leading case of *Card Protection Plan* C-349/96 must be referred to; this case tells us that whether there is a single supply must be considered from an economic point of view. If there is, the supply should not be artificially split. We therefore need to identify the essential features of the transaction when the taxpayer is making its supplies to its customer. The House of Lords found that the College was making an exempt supply of education which students took in order to gain qualifications. The provision of textbooks was a part of that exempt course of study.

It is clear, therefore, that we need to have learning material – whether online or printed – that is an essential part of a larger supply of eligible education in order for the exemption to be applied.

Vocational training

Vocational training means:

> "training or re-training or the provision of work experience for
>
> a) Any trade, profession or employment, or
> b) Any voluntary work connected with
>   a. Education, health , safety, or welfare, or
>   b. The carrying out of activities of a charitable nature"

HMRC's Education Notice states:

> Vocational training occurs where trainees attend courses, conferences, lectures, workshops or seminars and the purpose is to:
>
> - prepare for future employment
> - add to their knowledge to improve their performance in their current work
>
> Vocational training does not occur where (through counselling, business advice or consultancy) the purpose is to improve the working practices and efficiency of an organisation as a whole

Vocational training provided by an eligible body will be exempt, with the exception of vocational training provided by private schools from 1 January 2025 which will be standard rated.

Furthermore, vocational training provided by a non-eligible body will still be exempt where the provider is contracted (or subcontracted) under an approved governmental training scheme where the services are ultimately funded by

- the Department for Education (DfE)
- the apprenticeship service account (funded through the levy) to pay external providers for apprenticeship training
- the National Council for Education and Training for Wales
- a Local Enterprise Company
- the European Social Fund (under a scheme approved by the DfE)

Where the training is partly funded by the trainee or their employer, and partly from funds above, then the exemption will only apply to the extent that the government funding covers the charge with the remainder only being exempt if the training provider is an eligible body.

HMRC's current view is that vocational training must be strictly in relation to a particular trade, profession or employment, in order to be exempt and not general employment skills (such as careers advice, CV writing skills etc) which will fall to be standard rated.

Back in 2006, the Tribunal heard the case of *Creating Careers* (V19509) which concerned a Further Education college's partnering with Creating Careers to provide e-learning software packages. The taxpayer argued that it provided vocational training and therefore could exempt its supplies. Its online courses provided students the opportunity to earn an accredited qualification and each package was self-sufficient to enable students to achieve the qualification. The involvement of a live tutor was isolated to checking the learning is taking place and offering encouragement and pastoral support to students. The Tribunal found that the provision was clearly of more than just educational material, there was a complete package of education that required a considerable amount of learning time from the student, it was therefore an exempt supply of vocational learning.

Closely and non-closely related supplies

The exemption for education extends to cover "closely related" goods and services, as follows:

> "The supply of any goods or services (other than examination services) which are closely related to a supply of a description falling within....(the principal supply) by or to the eligible body making the principal supply provided—
>
> (a) the goods or services are for the direct use of the pupil, student or trainee (as the case may be) receiving the principal supply; and
>
> (b) where the supply is to the eligible body making the principal supply, it is made by another eligible body."

Importantly, private schools have been specifically permitted by HMRC to continue treating their closely related supplies as exempt, even though the primary education is now taxable.

A similar exemption applies to goods and services provided by the trainer that are essential to the provision of vocational training where that training is exempt under the provisions outlined above.

HMRC's Notice sets out that the following will be exempt if provided in relation to exempt education or vocational training:

- accommodation (except from 1 January 2025 board and lodging supplied by a private school or connected person)
- catering
- transport
- school trips
- field trips

HMRC gives the following examples of goods and services that are taxable in principle unless relief is available elsewhere:

- supplies to staff (including tutors on summer schools) and to other non-students
- sales of goods from school shops, campus shops and student bars
- sales from most vending machines
- sales of goods not needed for regular use in class
- separately charged laundry and other personal services
- sales of school uniforms and sports clothing
- admission charges (other than for taking part in sports activities) – for example, admission to plays, concerts, dances, sporting venues, exhibitions, museums and zoos – but *see* chapter 8 Cultural Exemptions
- administration and management services
- commission for allowing sales by outside organisations at an educational establishment
- sales by a sole proprietor or partnership in connection with private tuition

Except for closely related supplies between eligible bodies, there is no general exemption for goods and services supplied to providers of education, research and vocational training for use in their educational activities.

The closely related goods or services must be supplied directly to the students of the eligible body or to the students of another eligible body. Where the goods or services provided would otherwise be zero rated, such as textbooks, either exemption or zero rating can apply with zero rating being the obvious preference.

The more common closely related supplies (other than those mentioned by HMRC Education notice) are:

Books/printed material

These are likely to qualify for zero rate relief under Schedule 8, Group 3 and specifically Notice 701/10 references reference books and literary works as falling within the zero rate. School work books and other educational texts in question-and-answer format, are zero-rated because the spaces provided for the insertion of answers are incidental to the essential character of the book or booklet.

Stationery

Stationery supplied would otherwise be standard rated unless it qualifies as an exempt closely related supply.

Musical instruments

The hire of these is capable of being exempt as closely related supplies where charged for. The sale of instruments to a student will be exempt; for academies this should be a non-business activity provided charged at no more than cost.

Laptops

The case for laptops being "directly necessary" for the use of the student has not yet been addressed in the courts. Hence, for now, the hire or sale of laptops will be standard rated. Academies providing these at no more than cost can treat this as non-business.

Home to school transport

It is possible to zero rate passenger transport in a vehicle that has at least 10 seats, including for the driver and crew, where a fee is charged for the transportation. This affords recovery of costs directly attributable to the home to school transport services.

Many education providers operating this service have historically set this up through a special purpose vehicle (usually a subsidiary company) – see Chapter 14: TRADING SUBSIDIARIES – although the impetus for these arrangements has decreased following the changes introduced for private schools requiring them to now be VAT registered.

Uniform

Zero rating is available for clothing that meets specific sizing limits set out in Notice 714 on the basis that they are intended for children aged under 14. Even if those size restrictions are breached, zero rating can apply provided that the items are designed to fit a body no larger than those sizes or has features that restrict it to under 14s.

School hats that are specifically designed and held out for sale for children will also be zero rated.

Uniform is not otherwise subject to any general relief from standard rate.

Many education providers no longer sell uniform themselves but receive commission from a specified third party supplier. This commission will be standard rated.

Catering

HMRC accepts that catering provided to students will be closely related and therefore exempt when provided by an eligible body supplying exempt education.

In reality, applying this is not always straightforward not least because catering outlets are often utilised by non-students as well as students. This can be managed by identifying the status of buyers at the till point so that the split between exempt and standard rate sales can be reported, or by sampling the make up of buyers on a periodic basis and reporting the split on that basis. Most institutions will now have the ability to accurately identify any non-student meals sold at the till point.

Vending machines feature in many education establishments, even if the contents are changing to be more healthy in nature, and will generate income for the education provider. The VAT treatment of that income will depend upon the pricing of the products, the product being purchased and where the vending machine is situated.

HMRC manuals at VATEDU52000 advises that:

> "Food and drink supplied at or below cost from a tuck shop or vending machine run by a school takes on the same liability as the education."

Therefore, comments following relate only to sales of products at more than cost.

The liability of the product being sold will be determined by reference to the rules on food, found in Schedule 8, Group 1 and Public Notice 701/14. Case law on the intricacies of VAT on food is extensive and complex, but broadly the typical items dispensed from vending machines will be confectionary, crisps, soft drinks and hot drinks all of which are standard rated.

If the products being dispensed are potentially zero-rated food items, such as sandwiches, the location of the vending machine will need to be considered to determine the liability of its income. Vending machines located within the area of a canteen or restaurant will be seen as being providing standard rated catering. Income from machines located elsewhere, for example in corridors, will revert to the liability of the items being sold so potentially could include zero rated sales.

Alternatively, the education provider might be letting space to the vending machine provider in return for a rental income. In these circumstances, HMRC's current guidance indicates that providing space for a vending machine is subject to VAT, unless that machine forms part of a building or structure when it can be exempt (unless opted to tax).

HMRC has indicated that for private schools, the exemption afforded under the "closely related" provisions can be applied as long as meals are invoiced separate from charges for the taxable education. For boarders, the exemption is only extended to separately invoiced lunches supplied to students, and not to other meals that are provided as part of their board and lodging.

Academies

Academies are not "in business" for the purpose of providing education and their supplies of education are not therefore within the provisions of Group 6. That has the further implication that they cannot make use of the "closely related" relief for other goods and services provided to their students or to another eligible body's students.

Increasingly, academies are offering services outside their own trust to local authority schools and to other academy trusts. VAT may need to be charged on these supplies unless another relieving provision applies.

Supplies made to its own students can be treated as non-business supplies where they are either free or charged for at no more than cost. Supplies to students that are made at more than cost cannot benefit from the exemption provided for closely related supplies, with the income arising therefore being standard rated unless any other relieving provision applies.

Further Education colleges

Further Education colleges provide a mixture of business and non-business education. The closely related provisions apply only to the element of charged for (business) education whether provided to the college's own students or to students of another eligible body.

Supplies made to the college's own students can be treated as non-business supplies where they are free or charged for no more than cost.

The issue of what HMRC will accept as being "closely related" has been disputed over the years resulting in the lead decision of *R&C Commrs v Brockenhurst College* [2017] BVC 20. In this case, the taxpayer was a Further Education college providing a variety of educational courses including some that were vocational in nature and incorporated some aspects of practical application. The college's training restaurant and theatrical performances were found to be exempt as being closely related to supplies of education.

The issue was referred up to the ECJ, as was, and determined that three tests must be met in order for exemption to extend to these activities:

1. both the principal supply and the supplies of services closely related to it must be provided by bodies referred to in article 132(1)(i) of the Principal VAT Directive;
2. those supplies of services must be essential to the exempt activities; and
3. the basic purposes of those supplies of services must not be to obtain additional income for those bodies by carrying out transactions which directly compete with those of commercial enterprises which are liable for VAT.

These tests were further refined to include the requirement that the **basic purpose** of the activities must not be to obtain additional income through transactions that were in direct competition with commercial providers.

As a result, income arising from most vocational type activities of Further Education colleges should qualify to be treated as exempt being closely related to the supply of education. This would typically include income arising from: training restaurant, training hair or beauty salons, theatrical productions, animal grooming, garages offering car repairs etc. It will be essential for the provider to be both an eligible bodies for the provision of education, and for them to be able to evidence that the basic purpose of these activities is to provide a valuable and comprehensive education to students.

Private schools

Although fees and board are specifically removed from exemption for private schools, they are still able to benefit from the exemption for closely related supplies in respect of other items:

School meals

HMRC has accepted that lunches provided to students can be closely related and therefore exempt where they are charged for separate from the fee for education. If lunch is packaged up within school fees, it will be standard rated. Whether a school wishes to separately disclose the charge for its lunches will largely be a commercial decision.

Breakfast and evening meals provided to boarders will be standard rated as being ancillary to the supply of boarding.

School trips

Where these are taking place in the UK they may be either closely related and exempt where they are necessary for the course of education, or fall within the Tour Operators Margin Scheme (TOMS) where they are not. TOMS requires a particularly complex calculation to arrive at a margin to which VAT at the standard rate is applied. There is a general expectation that trips will generate no margin and therefore no VAT charge but it is necessary to confirm this by following the TOMS calculation rules as set out in Notice 709/5.

School trips that take place outside the UK will be zero rated.

Higher education

As eligible bodies supplying education, universities are able to exempt the provision of catering to their students. Strictly, this exemption does not extend to the provision of catering by student unions. However, by concession, HMRC will accept some exempting of catering supplied by student unions even though they are legally distinct from the university itself.

HMRC Notice 709/1 sets out when the supply of catering by student unions to students of the university can be treated as exempt. This specifies that the exemption will apply to catering to students from "canteens, refectories and other catering outlets (excluding bars), plus food and drink sold from vending machines situated in canteens and similar areas". Standard rate VAT will therefore need to be applied to sales of bar snacks and alcohol.

HMRC is currently challenging instances of the exemption being applied to sales from, in its view, bars by student unions. To date, this has only been considered in the *Anglia Ruskin Students' Union v HMRC* [2025] EWHC 296 case which resoundingly held that HMRC had acted reasonably in assessing sales from that union's venue, Bar 92, as being outside the concession and therefore standard rated.

Private tuition

Schedule 9 Group 6 Item 2 exempts:

> "the supply of private tuition, in a subject ordinarily taught in a school or university, by an individual teacher acting independently of an employer."

In order for the exemption to be applied, it is vital that both factors are present:

- tuition in a subject ordinarily taught in schools or universities, and
- supply by an individual acting on their own risk.

In reality, this means that exemption can only be applied under this item by a sole trader or by a partner in a partnership, but not by a limited company. This has the effect of precluding a private tuition business from achieving both VAT exemption and limiting its liabilities.

In *A & G Fahrschul-Akademie GmbH* (Case C-449/17), the Court of Justice held that school or university education generally referred to:

> "an integrated system for the transfer of knowledge and skills covering a wide and diversified set of subjects, and to the furthering and development of that knowledge and those skills by the pupils and students in the course of their progress and their specialisation in the various constituent stages of that system."

The ability to exempt activities depends upon a (rather wide) definition of the subjects that are ordinarily taught in schools or universities. A variety of cases have been taken to tribunal to decide whether the subject of the private tuition is ordinarily taught in schools and universities, or not. On the whole, HMRC is fairly generous in its interpretation but taxpayers have lost a number of cases which have found that the exemption is not applicable to pilates, yoga, belly dancing, motor cross instruction and maintenance. It is not sufficient for the subject to be taught infrequently in schools and universities. However, it is inevitable that over time the application of this definition will develop.

The case of *Marcus Webb Golf Professional v R&C Commrs* [2013] BVC 504 considered the scenario of an individual who was personally providing tuition but in fulfilment of contracts entered into by the company of which he was director, concluding that exemption could only be applied to the tuition he provided in his sole trader capacity, not as an employee of a company. The issue of whether this offended the principle of fiscal neutrality was considered but found that the Directive permitted differing liabilities depending upon the supplier, and had been correctly enacted into UK law.

Contrast this with *Haderer v Finanzamt Wilmersdorf* (Case C-445/05) which found that it was possible for the activities of the individual acting in a freelance capacity to be exempt provided that his activities consisted of private tuition in a subject within "school or university education", which was not the case here.

In an ECJ case *Eulitz* (C-473-08), confirms that an individual providing teaching for training courses that are offered by another body, cannot be supplying that training "privately" and therefore the VA exemption is not available for these supplies.

Examination services

Schedule 9, Group 6 Item 3 exempts:

> "the provision of examination services
> - By or to an eligible body, or
> - To a person receiving education or vocational training which is [exempt] or provided otherwise than in the course of furtherance of a business"

HMRC Notice 701/30 confirms that the following will be exempt:

- setting and marking examinations;
- setting educational or training standards;
- making assessments;
- other services provided with a view to ensuring that educational and training standard are maintained;
- services connected with GCSE and GCE examinations and National Curriculum tests;
- National Vocational Qualification (NVQ) assessments;
- course accreditation services;
- validation;
- certification (including issuing duplicates); and
- registering candidates.

This is quite a wide-ranging scope of examination services and clearly reflects the understanding that continuous assessment will fall within the exemption, as well as more traditional testing.

We know that the following services are not within the exemption:

- printers;
- graphic designers;
- typesetters;
- secretarial;
- advertising;
- promotional services; and
- public relations (PR) agents.

RM Education (V20911) considered the supply of e-marking services to an eligible body and whether these were exempt examination services. Here the Tribunal held that the e-marking service was not sufficiently close to the supply of examination services and therefore was not exempt. The recipient eligible body provided examination services and these were within the exemption, but its purchase of IT service to undertake marking were not.

Chapter 7: WELFARE EXEMPTION

Welfare services

Schedule 9, Group 7 provides that supplies of welfare services and connected goods by charities, state regulated private welfare institutions or agencies, or public bodies are exempt from VAT:

> "The supply by
> a) a charity
> b) a state-regulated private welfare institution [or agency],
> or
> c) a public body
> of welfare services and of goods supplied in connection with those welfare services."

Many schools and universities will have charitable status and will be able to supply exempt welfare services. For educational bodies that are not constituted as charities, these will likely still qualify as being "state regulated" due to being subject to Ofsted regulation.

HMRC acknowledges that: "after school clubs and other providers of non-residential care for children are only required to register under the appropriate social legislation if they provide a designated number of hours of care to children under the age of 8 years old. If you are a qualifying institution, you may, if you wish, choose to regard the care you provide to children over 8 years old as VAT exempt, in addition to the care you provide to younger children if you:

- provide care on a commercial basis to children who are younger than 8 years old, as well as to older children;
- operate identical hours of opening for all age groups; or
- provide activities for children over 8 years old that are comparable with those provided for younger children

Where an organisation does not fall within any of the criteria above, its provision of welfare services will be subject to VAT at the standard rate.

Exemption will then apply to eligible bodies that are providing:

- provision of care, treatment or instruction designed to promote the physical or mental welfare of elderly, sick, distressed or disabled persons;
- care or protection of children and young persons; or

- provision of spiritual welfare by a religious institution as part of a course of instruction or a retreat, which must not be designed primarily to provide recreation or a holiday.

Clearly, within the education sector, it will be the care or protection of children and young persons that is most relevant. Public Notice 701/2 confirms that exemption can apply to day care services such as those provided by a nursery, playgroup, or after school club (but not activity-based clubs such as dance classes).

Nursery provision

The operation of a nursery for children who are below compulsory school age will necessarily be supplied by an Ofsted regulated organisation, meaning that it is an eligible body providing care of children and can exempt its fees.

Exemption will extend to apply to the supply of meals and drinks for the children, as well as other sundry items provided as part of the children's care such as picture books, crayons and toys, provided that these form part of the exempt supply of welfare. Care needs to be taken if meals are offered as an optional extra as exemption might not apply to this income.

Many private schools operate nurseries and, since 1 January 2025, have had to ensure that nursery fees can all be VAT exempt. The current HMRC guidance specifies that a nursery class is exempt as long as 90% or more of the children are below compulsory school age at the time that the supply is made. Where a school operates mixed age classes, as is common within the Steiner school movement, the fees of the whole class can become subject to VAT at the standard rate if the 90% test is not met.

Initial complications that private school nurseries faced when invoicing Local Authorities for Early Years Funding seems to have largely resolved since the VAT changes on 1 January 2025. Where a school is invoicing for Early Years Funding from a Local Authority, VAT should be added where the child is of compulsory school age, rather than nursery age. Local Authorities are able to recover this VAT in full and so, theoretically, should not object to receiving a VAT invoice.

Before and after school clubs

The VAT liability of income from before and after school clubs was tested in the case of *RSR Sports Limited* (TC07450) which concerned the operation of school holiday camps by an organisation that is Ofsted regulated. The case held that their activities fell within the welfare exemption due to being predominantly childcare provision rather than activity-based. Subsequently, HMRC released Brief 18/2020 which set out its position. HMRC has accepted exemption applies to many organisations but does take a view that this is finely balanced and considers the key features for exemption to be:

- the members of the staff were merely supervising activities;
- they did not hold any teaching or coaching qualifications;
- there was no external standard to which the services were being provided; and
- the activities were merely an adjunct to the essential service which was childcare.

HMRC will look in detail at each of these aspects and, importantly, how the club is advertised to ensure that the predominant offering is of childcare, and not coaching.

From 1 January 2025, in private schools, the provision of clubs is standard rated where there is any element of teaching or instruction; this brings all sports clubs and homework clubs into the charge to tax unless the provision is clearly only of childcare, for example, provision of space to undertake prep but without any instruction being given.

It is clear that this is an area of potential dispute and therefore is important that the conditions set out in the HMRC Brief are closely adhered to in order to best protect the school's position.

Holiday clubs

As with before and after school clubs, holiday clubs can be exempt where the organisation is an eligible body and it is supplying childcare. Where the organisation is letting a third party provider use its facilities so that the third party can operate a holiday club, the VAT liability will largely be driven by rules applying to land and property, and these matters are covered in chapter 11.

Chapter 8: CULTURAL EXEMPTION

The cultural exemption applies to income arising from:

> "the supply by an eligible body of a right of admission to
> - A museum, gallery, art exhibition, or zoo, or
> - A theatrical, musical, or choreographic performance of a cultural nature"

An eligible body for these purposes is one that is:

1. precluded from distributing, and does not distribute, any profit it makes;
2. applies any profits made from supplies of a description falling [above], to the continuance or improvement of the facilities by means of the supplies; and
3. is managed and administered on a voluntary basis by persons who have no direct or indirect financial interest in its activities.

This exemption can prove useful where the educational organisation is receiving income from ticket sales to events.

Many events that are held will form a necessary part of the course of education for the students (for example, performances by drama students) and can therefore come within the education provision, for those that do not, the cultural exemption might apply to remove the default charge to VAT at the standard rate.

The conditions appear simple to meet, and are in many cases, but bear further scrutiny before reliance is placed upon them.

Precluded from distributing profit

The articles of association of the organisation will confirm whether it is able to distribute its profits or not and will largely be a matter of fact.

Applying profits to facilities

This condition can be a little harder to confirm as it will rely upon how the organisation is operated. It should be possible to demonstrate that if there is any surplus arising from cultural events (acknowledging that it is unusual in most cases to make any surplus), it is ring-fenced back into future events. If any surplus becomes subsumed within general funds, this condition will not be met. Inclusion of a specific clause within the organisation's Articles to the effect that profits must be used in this way would be helpful to achieve exemption.

Managed and administered on a voluntary basis

This condition has seen the most dispute and case law. Notably, the *Zoological Society of London* (C-267/00) challenged HMRC's interpretation of the conditions for exemption as not in line with the EU legislation which required that this condition referred to:

- those persons designated to direct the body at its highest level according to the constitution, and
- those who in fact, take the decisions of last resort - especially in the financial area - and carry out the higher supervisory tasks.

As a result, HMRC policy was changed and its Manuals now confirm that:

> "Persons taking the decisions of last resort are those who take decisions regarding the direction of a body, particularly – but not exclusively – in the financial area, and undertake the higher supervisory tasks. They do not include those who merely execute the decisions of others. Therefore, where the decisions of a paid Chief Executive must be approved by the cultural body's board, comprised wholly of volunteer members, this will not in itself disqualify a body from exemption, provided that the Chief Executive is not a board member with voting rights in respect of the decisions of last resort."

To identify who it is that has the power to take decision of last resort, the constitution or articles of association should be considered but also what actually happens in the organisation, which could be evidenced by Board Minutes or similar.

Once identified, those decision makers must be confirmed to be acting in a voluntary capacity. They will have an actual financial interest in the organisation's activities only when:

- the person receives any payments for services supplied to the organisation above the market rate, paid as routine overheads, or the payments made are profit-related (whether below, at or above market rates); or
- there's a link between the payments and the person's participation in the direction of the organisation's activities.

What types of events the exemption covers has been tested in the ECJ in *British Film Institute C-592/15* with the organisation. The BFI had claimed that the exemption applied to ticket sales for film screenings and that income from these could be VAT exempt. However, the court decided that the UK had some discretion within the EU legislation as to what could be treated as "cultural", and therefore the BFI could not apply exemption to its activities by direct reference to EU law.

Chapter 9: SPORTS EXEMPTION

The VAT Act 1994 exempts three items within the sports exemption:

1. the grant of a right to enter a competition in sport or physical recreation where the consideration for the grant consists in money which is to be allocated wholly towards the provision of a prize or prizes awarded in that competition;
2. the grant, by an eligible body established for the purposes of sport or physical recreation, of a right to enter a competition in such an activity; and
3. the supply by an eligible body to an individual of services closely linked with and essential to sport or physical education in which the individual is taking part.

These afford exemption on income arising from sports competitions but, more commonly for education organisations, supplies essential to an individual taking part in sport. For private schools, note that any sports education/training supplied will now no longer benefit from exemption since legislative changes from 1 January 2025.

Activities that are considered to be sports or physical education for the purposes of this exemption are wide-ranging and set out by HMRC within Public Notice 701/45:

Aikido	Gymnastics	Roller Hockey
American Football	Handball	Roller Skating
Angling	Hang or Para Gliding	Rounders
Archery	Highland Games	Rowing
Arm Wrestling	Hockey	Rugby League
Association Football	Horse Racing	Rugby Union
Athletics	Hovering	Sailing or yachting (includes canal cruising)
Badminton	Hurling	Sand and Land Yachting
Ballooning	Ice Hockey	Shinty
Baseball	Ice Skating	Shooting

Basketball	Jet Skiing	Skateboarding
Baton Twirling	Jiu Jitsu	Skiing
Biathlon	Judo	Skipping
Bicycle Polo	Kabaddi	Snooker
Billiards	Karate	Snowboarding
Bobsleigh	Kendo	Softball
Boccia	Korfball	Sombo or Sambo Wrestling
Bowls	Lacrosse	Squash
Boxing	Lawn Tennis	Stoolball
Camogie	Life Saving	Street Hockey
Canoeing	Luge	Sub-Aqua
Caving	Modern Pentathlon	Surf Life Saving
Chinese Martial Arts	Motor Cycling	Surfing
Cricket	Motor Sports	Swimming
Croquet	Mountaineering	Table Tennis
Crossbow	Movement and Dance	Taekwondo
Curling	Netball	Tang Soo Do
Cycling	Octopush	Tchoukball
Dragon Boat Racing	Orienteering	Tenpin Bowling (includes skittles)
Dance	Parachuting	Trampolining
Darts	Pétanque	Triathlon
Equestrian	Polo	Tug of War
Exercise and Fitness	Pony Trekking	Unihoc
Fencing	Pool	Volleyball
Field Sports	Quoits	Water Skiing

Fives	Racketball	Weightlifting
Flying	Rackets	Wrestling
Gaelic Football	Racquetball	Yoga
Gliding	Rambling	
Golf	Real Tennis	

It is possible to write to HMRC to request consideration of any other sport not already listed. Such an approach to HMRC might be recommended where absolute clarity on a sport not listed above is required, and where the catch-all of "exercise and fitness" does not apply.

For items 2 and 3 of the sports exemption to apply, the organisation must be an "eligible body" defined for these purposes as:

> "a non-profit making body which:
>
> - is precluded from distributing any profit it makes, or is allowed to distribute any such profit by means only of distributions to a non-profit making body,
> - applies…any profits it makes from [items 2 and 3] to
> - the continuance or improvement of any facilities made available in or in connection with the making of [sports supplies], or
> - the purposes of a non-profit making body
> - is not subject to commercial influence"

Looking at the organisation's constitution and confirming that it has non-distribution clauses will be necessary. Determining that there is no commercial influence is a matter which HMRC has provided a decision table within Public Notice 701/45:

Step	Decision
1	On each occasion you make a charge for initial or renewal of playing subscriptions or make some other type of sports supply, decide which period is, for the purposes of that supply, the 'relevant period'. Go to step 2.
2	Was a 'relevant supply' made to you in the relevant period? Go to step 3.
3	Have you paid an 'emolument'? Go to step 4.

4	Does an 'agreement' exist for either or both of the following to take place after the end of the relevant period, namely, the making of a relevant supply to you or the payment by you of any emolument? Go to step 5.
5	If you have answered yes to any of the questions at steps 2, 3 or 4 go to step 6. If you have answered no to all of the questions at steps 2, 3 and 4 you are not under 'commercial influence'.
6	Was the relevant supply made by, an emolument paid to, or agreement made with a 'person associated' with you at that time it was made or paid? If yes, you are under commercial influence for that supply. If no, you are not under commercial influence for that supply.

The "relevant period" runs for the three years leading up to the time of the sports supply.

A "relevant supply" for the purposes of the commercial influence test is a grant of either any interest in or right over land or licence to occupy any land which at any time in the relevant period was or was expected to become sports land.

"Emoluments" includes salaries, fees, wages, perquisites and profits calculated by reference to the profits or income from the organisation's activities.

Once clear that the organisation meets the eligible body criteria, we need to check whether its activity will be within the sporting exemption, which covers services closely linked with, an essential to, sport or physical education:

- playing, competing, refereeing, umpiring, judging, coaching or training (but not attending as a spectator or involvement in administration);
- use of changing rooms, showers and playing equipment together with storage of equipment essential to the sporting activity;
- match fees charged by an eligible body for use of the playing facilities; and
- mooring, hangarage and use of workshop facilities (but not the use of parts, or the services of an engineer).

The *Canterbury Hockey* case (C-253/07) significantly expanded the application of the sports exemption. This case, heard by the ECJ, concerned the treatment of affiliation fees paid to governing bodies by member clubs which HMRC had previously restricted exemption to only those fees calculated on a per person basis; all other calculation methods would be standard rated. The decision of the ECJ prompted HMRC's Business Brief 15/2010 which confirmed that exemption should be applied more widely and extends to services supplied to corporate persons and to unincorporated associations, provided that the supplies are closely linked and essential to sport, that they are supplied by non-profit making organisations and the true beneficiaries are individuals taking part in sport. The sports exemption will apply where those condition are met and is likely to be the majority of cases.

Chapter 10: COST SHARING EXEMPTION

The cost sharing exemption was implemented into UK law from July 2012 after challenge from the European courts for failure to enact it in the UK.

The exemption is aimed at enabling two or more organisations that have exempt and/or non-business activities to work collaboratively without incurring additional VAT cost. The organisations involved are required to set up an independent entity, known as the cost sharing group (CSG), which then supplies them with certain services. Goods are not included within the cost sharing exemption.

Since June 2018, use of the cost sharing exemption has been restricted to organisations who engage in public interest activities, including education. In order for the exemption to apply:

1. there must be an independent group of persons, the CSG, supplying services to its members;
2. all the members must carry on a relevant activity that is exempt from VAT or that is not a business activity for VAT purposes;
3. the services supplied by the CSG, to which the exemption applies, must be directly necessary for a member's relevant exempt and/or non-business activity;
4. the CSG only recovers, from its members, their individual share of the expenses incurred by the CSG in making the exempt supplies to its members; and
5. the application of the exemption to the supplies made by the CSG to its members is not likely to cause a distortion of competition.

The CSG is then able to supply services to its members without charging VAT where it would ordinarily be due. For education organisations, a CSG can be beneficial for sharing back-office services (such as finance, HR, and other administrative services) or staff. If these were purchased in from any other third party, VAT at the standard rate would be incurred which is likely to be largely irrecoverable (unless the purchasing organisation is able to recover all the VAT, for example it is an academy). Without the CSG, the cost of this type of collaborative working can become prohibitive due to the additional 20% cost being incurred.

The cost sharing exemption as a relatively new provision has not been subject to very much case law, other than *West of Scotland Colleges*

Partnership [2014] TC 03746 which considered whether members had made exact reimbursement of their share of joint expenses. This decision emphasises that the CSG must be both implemented and operated in strict accordance with the requirements in order to maintain exemption in the long term.

Chapter 11: CAPITAL EXPENDITURE

Capital expenditure on land and property will often be one of the largest costs that an organisation invests in. The spend can bring a large amount of VAT into the organisation. So clarity as to how much VAT is due to be incurred and whether it is recoverable is vitally important.

Land and property is one of the most complex areas of VAT with a plethora of exceptions and nuanced rules. This is especially true in the educational sector because reliefs are sometimes available to organisations in the sector and VAT is often not recoverable in full.

Often, a purchase or construction work will result in expenditure that falls within the Capital Goods Scheme (see Chapter 5: CAPITAL GOODS SCHEME).

Buying or selling land or property

A supply of land is generally, by default, exempt for VAT purposes meaning that VAT is not charged on its sale and purchase unless the seller has taken the decision to opt to tax. Opting to tax is a two-stage process of making the decision and then of notifying that decision to HMRC within 30 days. By opting to tax the notifying person is making a commitment to HMRC that VAT at the standard rate will be accounted for on income arising from the land and will in return be able to recover VAT on costs incurred attributable to that land.

The requirement to notify HMRC of an option to tax came into effect in 1995, but there are still occasions occurring when an organisation realises that it has been charging VAT but has not made the required notification to HMRC. In these cases, it is possible to make a late notification of the option by providing evidence to HMRC of the decision being taken and that VAT has been accounted for on income arising from the land since the time of that decision.

VAT incurred on any purchase is only potentially recoverable if it has been correctly charged. With land or property acquisitions, requesting confirmation of whether the seller has opted to tax and, if so, evidence of the notification made to HMRC is strongly recommended before any contracts are signed.

Schedule 9 Group 1 sets out a list of exceptions to the general exempt treatment, as follows:

(a) the grant of the fee simple (being the freehold) in—

(i) a building which has not been completed and which is neither designed as a dwelling or number of dwellings nor intended for use solely for a relevant residential purpose or a relevant charitable purpose;

(ii) a new* building which is neither designed as a dwelling or number of dwellings nor intended for use solely for a relevant residential purpose or a relevant charitable purpose after the grant;

(iii) a civil engineering work which has not been completed;

(iv) a new* civil engineering work;

* *new here being completed less than three years old before the grant*

(c) the grant of any interest, right or licence consisting of a right to take game or fish unless at the time of the grant the grantor grants to the grantee the fee simple of the land over which the right to take game or fish is exercisable;

(d) the provision in an hotel, inn, boarding house or similar establishment of sleeping accommodation or of accommodation in rooms which are provided in conjunction with sleeping accommodation or for the purpose of a supply of catering;

(e) the grant of any interest in, right over or licence to occupy holiday accommodation;

(f) the provision of seasonal pitches for caravans, and the grant of facilities at caravan parks to persons for whom such pitches are provided;

(g) the provision of pitches for tents or of camping facilities;

(h) the grant of facilities for parking a vehicle;

(j) the grant of any right to fell and remove standing timber;

(k) the grant of facilities for housing, or storage of, an aircraft or for mooring, or storage of, a ship, boat or other vessel;

(ka) the grant of facilities for the self storage of goods;

(l) the grant of any right to occupy a box, seat or other accommodation at a sports ground, theatre, concert hall or other place of entertainment;

(m) the grant of facilities for playing any sport or participating in any physical recreation;

(ma) the grant of facilities to a person who uses the facilities wholly or mainly to supply hairdressing services; and

(n)the grant of any right, including—

(i) an equitable right,

(ii) a right under an option or right of pre-emption, or

(iii) in relation to land in Scotland, a personal right,

to call for or be granted an interest or right which would fall within any of paragraphs (a) or (c).

Of these, commonly, car parking facilities, letting space for storage and accommodation in hotel-like facilities will be income streams that educational organisations will need to subject to VAT at the standard rate.

The situation with purchasing property is largely the same, with some notable exceptions.

Zero rating applies to the first sale or long lease (being a lease capable of exceeding 21 years) of a new residential dwelling or building newly converted into a residential dwelling. This affords the seller full VAT recovery on their costs, but will still mean that VAT is not charged to the organisation purchasing.

Zero rating will also apply to the first sale or long lease of a building that is intended to be used for relevant residential purpose (RRP) or relevant charitable purpose (RCP) – see below for detail of the conditions applicable here.

Letting land or property

Leasing land or property will similarly, by default, be VAT exempt unless the lessor has notified an option to tax over the site, in which case VAT would be charged on rent.

Constructing a building

Construction services are by default standard rated with exceptions for:

> "A building designed as a dwelling or number of dwellings or intended for use solely as a relevant residential purpose or a relevant charitable purposes...
> Of any services related to the construction other than the services of an architect, surveyor or any person acting as a consultant or in a supervisory capacity."

If an educational organisation is contracting for construction of an RRP or RCP building, it will need to certify to the contractor or contractors that the building's use will meet the requirements to be VAT relieved. Incorrectly issuing a certificate can give rise to penalties equal to the VAT that was not originally charged so the conditions bear scrutiny before a certificate is issued.

That certificate is confirming that there is an intention that the building will be used solely for eligible RRP or RCP purposes for a ten-year period; solely here though is interpreted by HMRC as being at least 95% qualifying as either RRP or RCP use.

How the 95% qualifying use is calculated is not prescribed and just needs to produce a fair result that accurately reflects the use of the building and can be checked easily. Typical methods of measuring include by floorspace or by time of qualifying use.

It is generally advisable to seek specialist advice before a certificate is issued and perhaps before building designs are finalised so that the 95% test is not inadvertently breached.

Relevant Residential Purpose (RRP)

Since 2014, HMRC has accepted that RRP buildings can also be eligible dwellings for VAT relief purposes, but the purpose of the RRP relief is to extend the treatment of dwellings to similar buildings that would not necessarily meet the dwelling definition.

Schedule 8, group 5 sets out what use as a RRP means:

(a) a home or other institution providing residential accommodation for children;

(b) a home or other institution providing residential accommodation with personal care for persons in need of personal care by reason of old age, disablement, past or present dependence on alcohol or drugs or past or present mental disorder;

(c) a hospice;

(d) residential accommodation for students or school pupils;

(e) residential accommodation for members of any of the armed forces;

(f) a monastery, nunnery or similar establishment; or

(g) an institution which is the sole or main residence of at least 90 per cent of its residents,

except use as a hospital, prison or similar institution or an hotel, inn or similar establishment

For education organisation, point d, "residential accommodation for students or school pupils" will be most relevant where boarding accommodation is constructed for students, whilst keeping in mind that hotels or similar are specifically excluded from the relief.

HMRC's Construction Manual comments that "school pupil" is uncontroversial but that "student" requires further clarification:

> "The term 'student' in this context refers to a person undertaking a course of educational study or instruction. It covers any person who is receiving education or vocational training from a university (or a centrally funded Higher Education institution or a Further Education institution) or from any other supplier who is providing similar, or the same type of, education or vocational training to a similar, or the same, academic standard."

Specifically, HMRC would not consider summer schools that offer life-enhancing experiences or promote greater cultural or spiritual awareness but the subject matter of which falls into the category of hobbies or leisure interests as opposed to receiving educational or vocational training to an academic standard, will not qualify as "students". HMRC is looking for a high degree of academic content, connected with a qualification or providing an academic experience to students.

The occupation of the building by the students must be for them to pursue their studies, not for purely leisure or other activities.

It is commonplace for student accommodation to be let for commercial use during holiday periods, often for conferences. This needs to be taken into consideration with respect to the 95% test. Lettings for student use where individuals are on a course of study should still be RRP qualifying, but lettings for conferences that are not part of a course of study will not qualify and need to be within the 5% tolerance to maintain RRP.

Universities could rely upon a concession up until April 2015 that permitted leeway on vacation lettings, but since that time, RRP treatment could only be used if expected use by non-students was confined to the 5% limit. However, depending upon the building design, many university accommodation blocks could qualify for zero rating on their construction as being "dwellings", but that would not extend to non-residential elements, meaning that the planning considerations become even more important if construction is to be bought in VAT-free.

Private schools and Higher Education providers constructing accommodation for boarding students should be able to secure zero rating but with the same consideration for vacation lettings and other non-qualifying use, and with attention to the design of the building.

Relevant Charitable Purpose (RCP)

In order for construction of a building to qualify for zero rating under the RCP heading Schedule 5, group 6 tells us:

> Use for a relevant charitable purpose means use by a charity in either or both the following ways, namely—
>
> (a) otherwise than in the course or furtherance of a business;
>
> (b) as a village hall or similarly in providing social or recreational facilities for a local community.

An educational organisation that has non-business activities would be able to issue a certificate to confirm its intended use of the building for qualifying RCP and remove VAT from its construction; this is most likely to be pertinent for academies and for Further Education providers (subject to developments post-Colchester Institute Corporation decision).

The distinction between business and non-business is set out above but, typically, organisations will have both types of activities and achieving RCP might mean ring-fencing a new building to one type of activity so that VAT relief on construction is achieved.

For Academies, RCP should be relatively easy to achieve given that the core educational provision is non-business and only occasional commercial use would be problematic and likely manageable within the 5% constraint.

Teaching space in Higher Education is unlikely to qualify for RCP relief given that this education is a business activity. However, a new university laboratory constructed for grant-funded research should be capable of RCP qualification but its use over the ten year period will need close monitoring to ensure commercial research activities are within the 5% limit.

Further Education providers have a more challenging task to construct an RCP building given that not all students will be grant-funded, but this should still be possible for sixth-form colleges and for others where it is practically possibly to restrict use of the new building to at least 95% grant-funded students. The question of whether RCP will be available at all to the Further Education sector remains in doubt following the Colchester Institute Corporation decision, unless and until clarification is provided by HMRC.

Change of use

Where an RRP or RCP certificate has been issued and construction received VAT-free, that building must remain within qualifying use for a period of ten years. A self-supply charge may arise if the building is sold or its use becomes non-qualifying in the ten years from its first use or practical completion, this takes the form of an output tax charge arising at the standard rate, effectively putting the owner back into the same position it would have been had VAT relief not been given. If the value of this output tax charge is sufficiently high, it might lead to the organisation having to VAT register simply because of the change of use of its certified building. If the self-supply charge is very large, it might create a Capital Goods Scheme asset that will need to be monitored (see chapter 5).

Whether the VAT arising on the self-supply charge is recoverable by the organisation depends upon what the building is then being used for.

Letting the qualifying building to a third party may not necessarily represent a change of use, if their use is itself qualifying, but somehow the owner must ensure that they know what a tenant will be using the property for in order to identify whether a self-supply charge has arisen, or not. There might therefore need to be requirements within the tenancy to restrict the activities of the tenant and/or to keep the owner informed as to the use of the property. If a self-supply charge does arise on letting to a third party, that VAT would be recoverable by the owner if the letting income was standard rated due to the owner having opted to tax.

Selling an RRP or RCP certified building will also give rise to a self-supply charge if the sale takes place within the ten-year monitoring period. As with letting, the self-supply VAT that arises might be recoverable if the sale itself were taxable e.g. because the property was opted to tax.

Whether sale and leaseback arrangements crystallise a self-supply charge was considered in the case of *Balhousie Holdings Limited v HMRC* [2021] UKSC 11 with HMRC's subsequent response to that decision set out in Business Brief 13/2021. Advice should be taken if such arrangements are being contemplated but suffice to say that it is possible that there will be no disposal for self-supply (or CGS) purposes in certain circumstances.

Chapter 12: VAT RELIEFS

Probably the most valuable relief often available to educational organisations is the zero rating of new builds covered in chapter 11. However, there are limited other reliefs that might be applicable to an organisation, as set out below:

Fuel and power

VAT at 5% (the reduced rate) rather than the standard rate is charged on gas, electricity, and solid fuels where used for domestic use, non-business activities, or small quantities. The supplier will charge VAT at 5% on qualifying bills. Where there is mixed use of the power, the supplier will need a certificate to tell them how much is qualifying for the reduced rate.

Where the power qualifies for the reduced rate, that relief will also extend to:

- disconnection and re-connection of the supply and special meter readings at the instigation of the supplier;
- installation by a supplier of liquefied petroleum gas of a bulk gas tank regarded as essential to the supply of liquefied petroleum gas;
- installation of check meters;
- installation or replacement of lines and switchgear belonging to the electricity supplier;
- installation tests and re-tests where required by the supplier to protect their equipment;
- maximum demand and minimum guarantee charges;
- removal of damaged coins or tokens from meters;
- rental charges for meters, including secondary meters used by landlords to apportion charges between their tenants;
- rental of a bulk gas tank in conjunction with the supply of liquefied petroleum gas to that tank;
- repair, maintenance or replacement of equipment and gas pipes or electric cables (belonging to the supplier) up to and including the consumer's meter;

- replacing a credit meter with a pre-payment meter under the supplier's Code of Practice, or replacing or re-siting by a supplier of their meter at their instigation;
- replacement of mains fuses and provisions of earthing terminals; and
- standing charges.

Qualifying use means either domestic use or charity non-business use. Any staff or student accommodation will therefore be able to receive fuel and power at the reduced rate. Charitable non-business use may also reduce standard rate VAT for academies as these are not in business for the provision of education, and possibly for research facilities of universities where these are not commercial but are grant-funded.

Even if the use is not entirely qualifying, the reduced rate will still be charged on the whole bill where 60% or more of the fuel or power is for qualifying use. If qualifying use is less than 60%, the reduced rate is charged only on the qualifying proportion, with the standard rate applying to the non-qualifying proportion.

Advertising

Charities can buy in advertising at the zero rate where they notify the supplier of their qualifying status. A charity for these purposes is limited to bodies that are registered, excepted, or exempted from registration with the Charity Commission, or bodies that are accepted by HMRC as charitable. Therefore, private schools, academies, Further Education colleges, and universities are likely to be able to benefit from this relief.

Traditional advertising on television, radio, newspapers etc is covered by the zero rating, but the extent of relief available to online advertising is more restrictive. Advertising on the organisation's own website will not qualify, but advertising on a third party website would. Where there is an element of audience selection though, HMRC has a limited definition of what will qualify. Currently, HMRC accepts that zero rating will apply to:

- audience targeting;
- behavioural targeting;
- channel targeting;
- content targeting;

- daypart targeting;
- demographic targeting;
- device targeting;
- direct placements on third party websites;
- location targeting;
- lookalike targeting;
- pay-per click advertising; and
- retargeting.

Where the advertising qualifies, the zero rate will extend to design and production of the advertisement.

Medical and research goods

Research institutions, such as universities, can purchase scientific equipment at the zero rate where those items are to be used in a non-business activity. The basic conditions for zero rating are:

1. the goods and services are purchased either by an eligible body or for donation to an eligible body;
2. the supply is either of qualifying goods or services or the repair and maintenance of qualifying goods;
3. If the supply is of medical, scientific, computer, video, sterilising, laboratory, or refrigeration equipment, this equipment is being purchased to be used by an eligible body mainly for medical or veterinary research, training, diagnosis or treatment;
4. Where the goods or services are being purchased by an eligible body, they are paid for using charitable or donated funds; and
5. The purchaser provides the supplier with a valid declaration of eligibility.

"Equipment" covers a wide range of items including:

- lab coats, scrubs, PPE;
- medical equipment that is designed for the diagnosis or treatment of patients, or the training of medical or veterinary professionals; and
- the following where used mainly for medical or veterinary research, training, diagnosis or treatment:

- scientific equipment designed to perform a scientific function, including precision measuring equipment and analytical equipment
- computer equipment
- video equipment
- sterilising equipment
- laboratory equipment such as test tubes, Bunsen burners, fume cupboards benches etc
- refrigeration equipment

HMRC Public Notice 701/6 provides further information about the extent of zero rating.

For the purchase to qualify, the funds to pay for the goods must be charitable or from voluntary donations or contributions.

Chapter 13: INTERNATIONAL ASPECTS

The majority of education organisations are unlikely to ever make supplies outside the confines of the UK. However, it is still important to have an understanding of the rules governing cross-border transactions as these inform which country has the taxing rights over the income.

As with many aspects of VAT, a good starting point is to establish whether you are considering "goods" or "services" as the regime are different for each. Schedule 4, Paragraph 1 references that goods involve:

> "the transfer of the whole property in goods as a supply of goods"

Anything else is regarded as "services". As a rule of thumb, goods will be tangible items over which ownership is transferred. Services will be generally intangibles and also goods where ownership does not change e.g. there is a lease.

Services

These provisions apply in the context of the UK organisation that is purchasing services from a supplier that is established outside the UK (or outside the EU in pre-Brexit periods). The CJEU case of *Wellcome Trust Limited* C-459/19 considered whether the reverse charge mechanism applies when services are being bought in by a VAT registered organisation for its non-economic activity and held that even Article 44 of the Principal VAT Directive must be interpreted as meaning that a VAT registered person which carries out a non-economic business activity must be regarded as 'a taxable person acting as such' when it acquires services from outside the EU (now outside the UK) for the purposes of that activity. As a result, Wellcome Trust and other VAT registered organisations cannot distinguish between times when they are buying in services from abroad for their business or their non-business activities, all must be subject to the reverse charge.

The general position is that supplies made:

By an organisation in business to another business	Place of supply is the country where the **receiving** business is established
By an organisation in business to a person not in business	Place of supply is the country where the **supplying** business is established

Many in the sector are venturing overseas to attract either students from abroad or to set up out partnerships or franchises abroad. Where the UK education organisation is making charges to an overseas business, it will not charge UK VAT, but will still include this income within its UK VAT return as a Box 6 value.

The flipside of this is that a UK organisation that is receiving supplies from a non-UK business also needs to consider the above rules. Knowing whether your organisation is purchasing services from abroad is vital as you will need to account for UK VAT on these and, if your organisation is currently not registered, the value of these purchases will count towards the registration threshold; this is due to what is known as the "reverse charge" mechanism.

For a UK organisation buying services from abroad these will, under the general rule set out above, be subject to the VAT rules of the country where the receiving organisation is established, being the UK. In some way, therefore, we need a mechanism to ensure that this supply is taxed in the UK and this is where the reverse charge applies. This situation commonly arises with private schools and universities utilising overseas agents to source students for them, as well as with social media, and with some IT licensing provision.

EXAMPLE:

A UK private school using social media to advertise for students. The social media provider is established in the United States.

It pays £1,000 per month to the US supplier and is therefore receiving services from abroad which are deemed to have a place of supply of the UK. Social media services are taxed at the standard rate of VAT in the UK, so are taxable.

Either, if it is not VAT registered, the college needs to add the £1,000 per month to its running total of taxable income to check whether it breaches the registration threshold,

Or, if it is already VAT registered, it needs to include the £1,000 per month in its VAT return under the reverse charge mechanism (see below).

Social media and IT services are two of the most common services purchased from non-UK suppliers, but there might be others, and these need to be identified so that correct reporting can be undertaken. An analysis of suppliers and identifying coding applied to the purchase ledger reporting should assist with reporting.

Reverse charge

The methodology for subjecting non-UK purchases to UK VAT is known as the reverse charge. This mechanism requires that the purchaser treats the transaction as being both a supply and a purchase. Continuing the example above:

Box 1: output tax @20%	£200 (payable to HMRC)
Box 4: input tax recoverable	£200 (recoverable from HMRC)
Box 6: net value of sale	£1,000
Box 7: net value of purchase	£1,000

In this example, there is a nil net overall effect. That would not be the case though where the UK organisation is not able to recover in full all the VAT that it incurs and this is reflected within its Box 4 entry (see chapter 11 Partial Exemption).

Goods

Goods that are purchased and imported into the UK are subject to some of the biggest post-Brexit changes. Imports into the UK are subject to UK import VAT at the time of entry and may also be subject to Customs Duty, depending upon a combination of factors.

In order to import goods, the organisation must have an EORI (economic operators registration and identification) number and this is easily obtained via HMRC's website but can take up to five days to be generated so needs to be planned in advance.

The VAT that is applied on imports will be the rate of VAT that would be due on those goods if sold in the UK. For the importer it is possible to recover that import VAT placing the imported goods on a level playing field with the same goods bought from a UK supplier. Customs Duty, if incurred, is not recoverable and will increase the price of the imported goods.

The ability to recover import VAT on goods depends upon two factors:

- having ownership of the goods at the time of import **and**
- being named on importation documentation as the importer.

HMRC has become particularly stringent on the first condition, challenging circumstances when import VAT has been claimed.

Provided that both conditions are met, the organisation must hold either a C79 certificate or a PVA statement. C79 certificates are issued monthly by HMRC and show all the imports and import VAT paid by that organisation identified by their EORI number. Postponed VAT Accounting (PVA) statements are downloaded from the Customs Declaration Service. Both documents provide the evidence required to report import VAT and recover this in the same way that an invoice from a UK supplier would be.

A C79 certificate will show how much VAT is potential able to be recovered within Box 4 of the UK VAT return.

A PVA statement shows entries to include in Box 1 (as output VAT to be paid), Box 4 (the recoverable amount calculated bearing partial exemption in mind), and the Net value within Box 7. The advantage of utilising PVA is that there is no cashflow impact arising from the delay between paying the import VAT and recovering it within the UK VAT return, whereas ordinarily, the import VAT is paid at the time of import for recovery later. PVA is not, however, available for organisations importing for wholly non-business activities; in these circumstances the import VAT must be paid on import and a proportion (if any) recovered later via the UK VAT return.

Operating outside the UK

VAT will be only one consideration if your organisation is looking to begin activities outside the UK and specialist advice is always necessary to ensure that plans are fully compliant. The extent to which the organisation steps into the overseas market is a sliding scale and could simply be allowing overseas attendees at an event through to setting up a new entity outside the UK.

Commentary on the more common scenarios follows but it warrants reiteration that bespoke advice pertinent to your organisation is worth obtaining.

Conferences and other events are an obvious way in which an organisation can stray into international aspects. The general place of supply rules set out above have some exceptions, one of which applies to the admission to events. Where an organisation is providing admission to an event to either businesses or consumers, the place of supply will be where that event is taking place and local VAT rules will apply. This means that a UK based event will charge VAT on its admissions income (unless the cultural exemption applies) even when attendees are themselves not UK established. Likewise, an event that is organised outside the UK (particularly in the EU) is likely to require a local VAT registration and that local VAT is charged to attendees but this can vary from country to country such that local advice should be taken.

A conference or exhibition event held in the UK at which non-UK exhibitors pay to attend will be treated as a land-based supply if the exhibitor is given a specific are at which to exhibit without any other services. HMRC Business Brief 22/2012 provides helpful clarity on exhibition and conference stand space, summarised as:

- organisers are making a supply of land where 'the service is restricted to the mere supply of space without any accompanying services'. In this case the place of supply is where the land is situated; and
- where stand space is provided with accompanying services as a package' the organiser is not making a supply of land. The 'accompany service' includes things as 'the design and erection of a temporary stand, security, power, telecommunications, hire of machinery or publicity material'. In this case the service is taxed under the general rule" (i.e. dependent upon whether this is a B2B or a B2C supply).

Where the organisation is making a land-based supply, the place of supply will always be where the land is situated and will generate exempt income for the organisation unless it has opted to tax the land (or is running the event as an exempt fundraising event).

Online events

The prevalence of online events rose during the Covid years but continue to be popular due to their ability to reach further afield than a local audience. Where an event draws in attendees from outside the UK, a plethora of possible treatments can arise.

The first consideration is whether the electronically supplied services rules apply and these will bite when, broadly, the online service is uploaded and then available to the recipient without further interaction e.g. online magazines. Simply using the internet to place orders or to fulfil orders will not bring these within the electronically supplied services rules. HMRC has confirmed within its "VAT rules if you supply digital services to private consumers" publication that educational or professional courses, where the content is delivered by a teacher over the internet or an electronic network (in other words, using a remote link) will not be treated as electronically supplied services.

Where the type of B2C service your organisation supplies falls into the electronically supplied services rules, the place of supply will be where each consumer is established potentially requiring multiple VAT registrations unless your organisation registers under the Mini One Stop Shop rules for its EU consumer supplies when just one return reports supplies made across the EU. For B2B electronically supplied services, the use and enjoyment rules may impact. The use and enjoyment rules apply in either of the following situations where the place of supply under the general rule would be:

- the UK but the services are effectively used and enjoyed outside the UK; or
- outside the UK but the services are effectively used and enjoyed in the UK.

In these circumstances, the place of supply is where the effective use and enjoyment take place. Where this is the UK, the services are subject to UK VAT.

If your organisation is considering a move into online events, you will need to identify whether this will be a B2B or a B2C activity and whether it falls within the electronically supplied services rules, in order to ensure that VAT reporting is correct.

Chapter 14: TRADING SUBSIDIARIES

Many educational organisations have a subsidiary company (or companies) that will undertake some of their activities. There are many reasons why this structure exists including, for example, to ring-fence potentially higher risk activities in a limited liability entity, to operate non-educational activities, or to remove non-primary purpose trading from a charity which risks the charity becoming subject to corporation tax.

The VAT profile of a subsidiary company needs to be considered on its own in order to determine whether it needs to be VAT registered. If it does VAT register, it will be given its own VAT registration number and be required to file its own VAT returns. Any transactions between the subsidiary and the parent organisation will take the usual VAT treatment and it is important to ensure that VAT is charged and recovered appropriately on any supplies made between the two registrations and that invoices are in the correct entity's name. This is all true unless the subsidiary and education organisation create a VAT group registration.

In order to form a VAT group registration the entities must:

- be established in the UK
- satisfy the control test:
    - one of them controls each of the others
    - one person (whether a body corporate or an individual) controls all of them, or
    - two or more individuals carrying on a business control all of them
- they satisfy anti-avoidance provisions

"Control" for these purposes refers to the Companies Act 2006 definitions but, broadly, means having the majority of voting rights or the right to appoint or remove a majority of its directors.

There are specific anti-avoidance measures allowing HMRC to refuse a VAT group registration application in certain circumstances; these rarely impact the education sector but do need to be considered ahead of an application.

Once a VAT group registration is in place, only one VAT return is prepared and submitted for all of the group's members. Any transactions that take place between members of the VAT group are disregarded for VAT purposes, meaning that no VAT is charged on intra-group supplies. This removes the need to consider the liability of any supplies made between the group members.

The downside of a VAT group registration is that the members are jointly and severally liable for the registration's VAT, the partial exemption *de minimis* limits apply across the group as a whole, the error notification limits apply across the group so are more likely to be breached, limits such as the payments on account limit apply across the group so a group registration with large VAT payments is more likely to be required to make payments on account. These factors need to be considered before an application to group is submitted.

Typically, a subsidiary will make use of at least some of the assets of the educational organisation, whether that be its properties, its staff, or its administrative systems. Especially where the organisation is a charity, it will need to consider carefully what charges it should make to its subsidiary to ensure that the charity's assets are not improperly used to support a non-charitable entity. Where a VAT group is in place, these charges will not bear VAT, in other cases the VAT treatment needs to be determined and VAT accounted for accordingly.

One of the main ways that a trading subsidiary will utilise the education organisation's assets is by operating letting of the property during holidays, for example to holiday club providers or to providers of tuition in English as a foreign language. There are a variety of ways that these arrangements can be structured with HMRC's internal manuals at VATEDU80000 providing a helpful overview of the treatment of these where a lease or licence has been granted to the subsidiary and:

1. the subsidiary then lets out the property together with catering – this will be a standard rated supply by the subsidiary;
2. the subsidiary grants licences to others to occupy the property together with providing catering, but passes the consideration received back to the educational organisation – there will be a supply by the educational organisation that could be exempt if the occupier is themselves an eligible body for the education exemption and the supply is closely related to their provision of education. Otherwise, standard rate VAT will be due;
3. the subsidiary grants licences to others to occupy the property together with providing catering, then donates the proceeds to the

educational organisation – standard rate VAT is due on the subsidiary's supply.

Other activities that a subsidiary might undertake include operating a retail outlet, providing consultancy services utilising the skills and reputation of senior leadership, or running external catering. With the exception of the scenario outlined above at 2, the trading subsidiary is unlikely to be an eligible body itself and will not therefore be able to take advantage of the exemptions that the educational organisation can use. This means that the VAT liability of the activities within the subsidiary will likely change compared to operation in the organisation, that will impact both the pricing set by the subsidiary but may also improve the VAT recovery of costs.

INDEX

www.ingramcontent.com/pod-product-compliance
Lightning Source LLC
LaVergne TN
LVHW050827061126
851857LV00012B/1020
9781913507909